The Bull of Heaven

*The Story of a Boy Who Grew Up
in a War Zone to Become a French
Stock Market Millionaire Fighting for
Shareholder Justice in North America*

BY
NAWAR ALSAADI

For my dad,
I love you and I miss you

TABLE OF CONTENTS

INTRODUCTION

I know, I know. I hate book introductions too. When I pick up a book, I often skip to the first chapter. But I now understand why authors write introductions. An introduction help put the story in the correct context; and it can help with navigating a complex and varied tale.

I have written this book to narrate a story, my life story. I didn't write it out of vanity, or for fame. I wrote it because I believe that my story can inspire people and motivate them to accomplish their dreams.

I don't know if my story will appeal to a wide audience, or to a specific audience—when my life was written, I didn't worry about an audience. And while a large section of this book deals with my business experience, this experience has been often coloured by my personal life; the professional and personal sides of my life have always been intertwined.

As you will see, I start by narrating my childhood in Baghdad during the Iraq-Iran war and the perils of living under a dictatorial regime. I then take you through my exile in Europe, my baby steps in the stock market, and my roller-coaster stock market ride during the technology boom of the late 1990s. Then we crash-land in Paris, as my world falls apart and my father is vanquished by cancer. From there, we fly to Canada, where I conquer the stock market and use my wealth to fight what I perceived to be corporate evil, in a battle that tested every fibre of my being.

When I first thought of writing this book, many people suggested that I write a 'how-to' book. But I don't think that life's lessons can be summarized in bullet points and easy-to-read paragraphs. Life is full of colour, and nuance. Life is subtle, life is hard, life is beautiful and life is unpredictable. I decided to tell the story as it happened, and let you decide if there is something to learn from it. If not, I hope you will at least find the experience of reading my story to be captivating and entertaining.

You will notice that each chapter starts with the name and lyrics of a song. My editor thought this didn't work with the book, but I strongly disagreed. Every song and lyric cited in my chapter headings is there because it inspired me. These songs coloured the chapters of my life, so it seemed fitting that they would be included within the pages of this book. As Friedrich Nietzsche said, "Without music, life would be a mistake".

Finally, I would like to take this opportunity to thank all of those who have helped make this book possible. You know who you are. From the bottom of my heart, thank you.

1

BANG BANG

Bang bang, I hit the ground
Bang bang, that awful sound

Cher

My first memories are of war. When I think back to the earliest event
I recall, to the oldest images that persist in my mind, I find an air raid.
I was two or three years old, and the Iranian air force was dropping
bombs on Baghdad. I was with my mother and older sister Tania in
the family room of our house, which we called the 'Red Living Room'
because it featured dark red furniture and a large red and blue mural
painted by my mother. My mother was holding me tightly, to soothe me,
but also as a way of controlling her own overwhelming terror. She was
a capable and resourceful woman, but she could also crumble under the
weight of anxiety, and it was often we children who had to comfort her,
rather than the other way around.

The room was dark. During air raids, electricity was cut to make
it harder for enemy planes to find their targets. Outside, the sun was
setting, and we could see the Iranian planes streaking through the early
evening sky as we prayed that they would spare our house. This night,

we were lucky. The Iranian pilots dropped their bombs a few kilometers away, and then turned back to Iran.

When I was two, in September 1980, Saddam Hussein invaded Iran with a simultaneous air and land assault. While the conflict had many roots, the position of the Iraqi regime, constantly repeated to the country's citizens, was simple: Iran was the enemy. Iranians were savage, bloodthirsty fundamentalists who would murder or enslave us if given the chance. The only option was to fight, and to win. This was a rather blunt and unsophisticated bit of propaganda certainly, but Iraqis were patriotic and they united to defend their homeland. When your country is at war, who started it does not matter.

For the first year, the war went well, with Iraq quickly conquering and controlling large areas of Iranian territory. The nightly news was filled with footage of victories and optimistic reports, and it seemed that Saddam Hussein might actually fulfill his dream of becoming the leader of a larger, unified empire spanning the Persian Gulf, or as we called it, the Arabian Gulf.

But by the end of 1981, the tide had started to turn. The Iranians became more organized, and started to push back with increasingly successful offensives. Iran had a much larger population (40 million Iranians compared to 14 million Iraqis), and was able to employ the shocking but effective tactic of the 'human wave'. It was simple: Iranian generals would order enormous numbers of men to march on the Iraqi lines. Row upon row of soldiers would be slaughtered, and the Iraqis would be overwhelmed by sheer numbers. The casualties were staggering. But the tactic was successful. It had the effect of halting further Iraqi advances, and it made the commanders in Baghdad realize that they were facing a formidable enemy—and a fanatical army. The corpses of Iranian soldiers were often wearing necklaces with plastic keys on them: these were the 'keys to heaven', which would allow them to enter paradise as a reward for sacrificing themselves for their ayatollah and their god.

By June 1982, the Iraqi army was on the defensive. Iranian offenses battered Saddam's military and forced numerous retreats. Faced for the first time with the possibility of losing the war, Saddam sued for peace, declaring a ceasefire and offering to recognize the borders that existed before the war. The Iranian government refused this offer, so the war continued for a further six years, with casualties and atrocities mounting on both sides.

The later years of the war, from 1983 to 1988, were similar to World War I in Europe. Both armies maintained huge systems of trenches, and fighting bogged down for years. A desolate No Man's Land often stretched between the fronts, and chemical weapons and gas were used in an attempt to gain advantage and break the stalemate. It was a brutal, bloody conflict that, in the end, achieved absolutely nothing. When the fighting finally stopped, in 1988, the border between the two countries was exactly the same as it had been eight years previous, yet as many as 1.25 million people died in the exercise according to the Correlates of War project.

As a child growing up in Baghdad, the war was never far away. Baghdad is just 120 kilometres (75 miles) from the Iranian border, which meant that if our front lines were to break, a single strong Iranian offensive could quickly flood the city with enemy combatants. I was aware of this at all times and this constant underlying fear imparted an edge of stress to daily life. I had recurring nightmares of an invasion, which we all thought would surely come if our army could not defeat the enemy. Of course, the official government position was that Iranian defeat was assured, but this propaganda did little to assuage the persistent fear that we could, or would, be invaded.

Even greater than the threat of a ground invasion was the constant fear of attack from above. As both the capital and the chief population centre of Iraq, Baghdad was one of Tehran's primary targets for bomb-ings and missile launches. During the middle and latter years of the conflict, from 1985 to 1988, we lived through what was called 'The War of the Cities', with both sides launching endless aerial raids on strate-gic targets, as well as numerous bombing attacks and SCUD missile launches against non-combatant populations.

Later, I learned that the Iranians bore the brunt of this civilian death and destruction. The Iraqi military was better supplied, with arms from the Soviet Union and France and strategic assistance from the United States. Saddam had vowed that for every Iranian bomb that fell on our country, he would send ten back in the other direction, and he had the firepower to back up his threat.

Of course, both sides viewed every missile launch as 'retaliatory', and both sides felt justified in responding to the other's most recent strike. It was a self-perpetuating cycle of revenge and insanity, and we were never more alert than just after Iraq fired missiles at Iranian cities, because we knew that Tehran would swiftly answer. Often, when we heard about our side launching an attack, we would leave the city for a few days, to stay with relatives in the suburbs and, hopefully, be far from the destruction of the enemy's response.

The war was essentially a decade-long stalemate. And there was psychological torture involved, because the fighting was not constant. Short periods of intense combat were separated by long intervals with little or no fighting, and weeks or months could go by without an air raid on Baghdad. These breaks lulled us into a false complacency, allowing us to concentrate on ordinary things like schoolwork, gro-cery lists and taking short trips to one of the tourist lakes north of Baghdad. Then, out of the blue, the air raid sirens would start shriek-ing, the lights would go out, and the ground would shake with the impact of nearby detonations. The fear that we had all repressed would, once again leap to the surface.

I remember one particularly terrifying night of aerial bombing, during the time my father was in prison (more on that later). To give us a break from the tension, my mother took us out for dessert. We left my baby sister Tamara in the care of my grandmother, and took a taxi to an ice cream shop in the popular commercial district of Al Mansour. For a few hours, the evening was idyllic and relaxing. We walked among the shops and restaurants, ate our ice cream, talked, laughed and generally enjoyed ourselves. The fighting and killing seemed a long way off and the city seemed at peace.

Then, in an instant, our happiness was shattered by the sound of a massive explosion coming from the direction of our neighbourhood, Al Qadsia. A hundred gruesome images flashed through our minds at once. Had Grandma and Tamara been hit by flying glass as the explosion blew in our windows? Were they pinned beneath rubble? Was our house a smoldering crater? We had to get home. We managed to convince a taxi driver to take us in the direction of the explosion. As we got closer to home, we saw a huge billowing column of black smoke ascending to the sky.

My heart raced as we turned onto our street. There was no electricity and the street was blacked out, but we found our house. It was still standing, albeit without windows. Grandma and Tamara were safe. We embraced, relieved and thankful to be spared, knowing that many other families in our neighbourhood could not say the same. A few streets away, people we saw every day in the shops, or at school, were dead. Men, women and children had been blown to pieces by an explosives-filled missile bought from the USSR and sold to Iran by Libya or Syria (the only two Arab countries who sided with Iran during the war and supplied it with weapons), and launched into our neighbourhood with no knowledge of, or concern for, the Iraqis it would kill.

Iraqis are amazingly adept at adapting to difficult circumstances. Despite years of war and tension, life went on in Baghdad. People spent their evenings in cafes, restaurants, cinemas, bars and even nightclubs; despite all its faults, the Ba'ath Party was secular in nature and allowed alcohol, mixed schools and revealing western-style clothing. Like millions of other people who have lived through times of war, we were all determined to stay alive and make the best of a bad situation.

I was just two years old when the war began but, as my parents told it, the early years of the conflict, from 1980 to 1982, were not significantly different from peacetime, except for the air raids. My father was working for the government, we had all the money we needed and there were few real shortages. The government was determined that the public would not feel the weight of the war, so it flooded the market with food, electronics, consumer products... anything to convince the populace that all was well and the fighting could progress without taxing the economy.

At first, many people were convinced the war would be short, lasting a few months at most. But by the fourth year, 1984, the war was taking a heavy toll. The nation was deeply in debt, the value of the Iraqi dinar had plummeted, and our middle class abundance was replaced with shortages. Things like butter and coffee became scarce, my father gave up drinking milk so there would be enough for Tania, and my grandmother would rise at 5:00 a.m. to stand in line for bread. My mother became adept at improvising delicious meals from spices and bits of meat and vegetables. She became so skilled at 'making do' that she published a cookbook showcasing her recipes and strategies. I spent many hours by her side as she cooked, amazed by her ingenuity and happy to help by performing any tasks she gave me. To this day, we share that connection, and I am often happiest when cooking something my mother taught me to make.

In times of shortages, certain items become precious to children. Any kid who could get his hands on a Mars bar or Kit-Kat was like a king among beggars. Kleenex was a rare find. We had limited access to locally-made tissues that felt like sandpaper to a runny-nosed kid like me. When the real thing appeared in the shops, I would hoard it, stashing it away like treasure. Long after we left Iraq, I feared running out of tissue and, to this day, I am careful to keep a good supply on hand. When your formative years are lived in a time of suffering and scarcity, old habits become difficult to break.

Still, we were better off than the families of many of the kids I knew. While Iraq and Iran fought their pointless and costly war, oil-rich Kuwait remained stable and prosperous. We had an uncle there who would send care packages, and I can remember sitting with my sister, carefully dividing pieces of Quality Street candy or "Mackintosh" as we called it, and setting some aside for my mother and grandmother. Our father rarely shared in the bounty as he was often absent.

■ ■ ■

The war was both omnipresent and absent, the backdrop of my existence. When children grow up in a time of war, they do not understand how bad things are, or that there is another way of living. Now, from the serenity of my apartment in Vancouver, I look back and remember the huge anti-aircraft gun mounted on the roof of my school and the black banner hung on my neighbour's house to tell us that a son or brother or father had been martyred. I would overhear my mother speaking of a cousin who went to the front and never came back, while the TV presented war footage and patriotic songs. These things were the facts of everyday Iraqi life in the 1980s.

Yet, I got on with the job of being a kid. There were books and comics, and cartoons on television. I had my friends, and I played all the games that young boys play. Because war was nearly always on our minds, play often took the form of war games and mock battles, either on the playground with improvised guns and bombs, or in our yards with toy soldiers, model planes and plastic tanks. We built elaborate battlefields in our garden, digging miniature trenches in the soil, lining up armies, and throwing lit fireplace matches as missiles. This omnipresent theme of war spilled over into my childhood drawings as I used my pencils and markers to draw speeding fighter planes, huge explosions and heroic soldiers.

The heat of the Iraqi summer brought other diversions. Baghdad is a hot city, with 320 annual days of sun and oppressive summer heat only occasionally relieved by sandstorms. As the desert sun blazes down, the streets feel like bricks in an enormous fireplace. We were lucky to have a small rubber wading pool, which my sister and I used for relief. Our laughter and splashing would attract other children and, as the body heat and sun raised the water temperature, the crowded pool became more like an outdoor Jacuzzi. Even better were the October rains that ended the summers. At the first sound of raindrops, Tania and I would run outside, joyously dancing and leaping through the cloudbursts.

Another vivid memory of summer in Baghdad is of sleeping on the roof of our house. The desert air does not hold heat well. Once the sun sets, the outside air cools rapidly, and many Iraqi families sleep on the flat roofs of their homes during the hottest months, particularly if the electricity is out and the air-conditioning is not working. This always felt like a bit of an adventure, like a camping trip. But the best part of sleeping up there was being able to look at the night sky. Baghdad is a large, sprawling city, yet there is minimal light pollution at night and the sky is nearly as clear as it is over the open desert. I remember lying on my back, staring up into the infinite reaches of space, seeing the curving arm of the Milky Way arching high above, losing myself in a million twinkling points of starlight. No other place I have lived in has had a sky so beautiful. The universe looked like a vast cloth of blackest velvet, strewn with shattered, glittering diamonds. This blanket of stars fascinated me, and ingrained in me a sense of wonder about the world and our place in the universe.

Throughout the war, my parents made sure that I didn't miss a day of school. And I did well. I don't remember studying particularly hard, but I was always the top student in my grade, and doing well motivated me to stay on top. I enjoyed math, science and history, and did so well that my teachers would pull me from the classroom to have me solve a math problem or answer a question for a class several grades higher— which, of course, would shame the older students into doing better.

Iraqi schools are very big on discipline. We were naturally required to wear uniforms. And every morning, we would stand rigidly in line and loudly recite the slogan of the Ba'ath Party: 'Unity, Liberty, Socialism!' On Thursdays, we had a ceremony to raise the flag. We sang the national anthem (*The Land of the Two Rivers*), and listened to long patriotic speeches about the progress and necessity of the war, and the noble goals of the Ba'ath Party. Also on Thursdays, students who had misbehaved would have their heads shaved, and the newly-bald would be displayed to the student body as examples of the consequences of angering the teachers. Few of us dared step out of line. Naturally, there were portraits of Saddam in every classroom, and every time a teacher walked in, we would stand up and say, "Long Live our President and Leader, Saddam Hussein!"

In 1989, when I was in the fifth grade, Iraq instituted 'The Ideal Student Program'. The idea was to identify and celebrate young people who embodied the best traits of humanity and who were, there-fore, reflections of that ultimate personification of perfection, Saddam Hussein. Every classroom in the country was required to hold a vote, with the students picking their 'ideal' classmate. I happened to be sick at home on the day of the voting, but I was elected anyway, in absentia. I was happy and wore my Ideal Student badge with pride. The following year, I won again and, this time, Ideal Students from around the country were scheduled to meet with Saddam. But the meeting never happened. That summer, Iraq invaded Kuwait, an action that had enormous consequences for the nation, and for my family.

I don't recall ever being bullied in school. This may have been because I was a respected student, or because the atmosphere of strict control cut down on bullying in general. The most likely reason is that my crazy aunt, my father's sister, was one of the school's math teachers. Aunt Jamila had a well-earned reputation as a mean and angry woman, prone to sudden outbursts of temper and violence—even sadism. Her preferred form of discipline was beating students with a stick. On one occasion, she called a young girl up to the blackboard to solve a math problem, and when the girl was unable to provide the answer, Jamila repeatedly pounded her head against the blackboard, until the girl's glasses fell to the floor and she wept uncontrollably, with my aunt still screaming at her to solve the problem. In another incident, she took the heavy metallic bell used to call students to class, and hit a boy so hard with it that he collapsed and had to go to hospital. In fact, my aunt had no particular love for me and was very hard on me. When my father was in prison, whenever I earned a grade other than 10 out of 10, she would pull me aside, berate me, and threaten to tell my father I was failing him. But I certainly wasn't going to tell the other students that my aunt was cruel to me; as long as they believed that the most feared teacher in the school was somehow looking out for her nephew, I was free from harassment.

When I was eleven, I developed a crush on one of my schoolmates. Zuhal was the most popular girl in my class, a Christian with fair hair and skin and large blue eyes. Zuhal was interested in me too. I also stood out. I had very white skin, fair hair, and looked more European than Iraqi. There were four non-Muslims in my class, including my best friend Taif. Non-Muslims were permitted to skip the Islamic Studies class, and we awaited eagerly for that time of the week, so we could leave the class with Zuhal and another Christian girl. But I was shy; aside from touching hands, our relationship remained platonic, although I thought I might one day marry her. I still wonder what happened to Zuhal; after I was stranded outside Iraq in 1990, I never heard of her again.

Not all of my education came from school. My mother was a writer and a painter, and I was immersed in the arts. I recall the hours spent at her studio, watching her carefully make her brush strokes; oil paint has a distinct smell, and whenever I come across it, I travel back in time to that studio.

My mother's paintings had gained her a fair measure of fame in Iraq—across the Arab world, in fact, and our family often attended art events and exhibitions. Baghdad had a vibrant arts scene and the regime rarely interfered with art (unless it was political), so we were exposed to a wide range of artistic styles. We also saw plenty of ancient art and artifacts from Mesopotamia's history as 'the Cradle of Civilization', and we went on tours of centuries-old ruins and other historic sites, such as the remains of the City of Babylon. Both my parents were proud of what our homeland had given the world, even as they were disturbed by what the Ba'ath regime had done to Iraq.

My parents took us to classical music performances and the ballet; I remember seeing *Swan Lake* for the first time at the Baghdad National Theatre. We had a piano, and Tania was a dedicated and gifted pianist; she began composing at age six, and was considered a prodigy. No matter how bad things got with the war, my parents made sure she continued with her piano lessons, and she kept on with them until our last days in Baghdad.

As is the case under any dictatorship, there was plenty of music and art created purely to glorify the regime and its leader. The certain appeal to the vanity of a ruler with a notoriously large ego is an easy way for an artist to curry favour and gain recognition. In 1990, I attended one particularly memorable exhibition, featuring nothing but portraits of

Saddam by the artist Nadith Saadi. The subject matter does not warrant discussion, as there were thousands of portraits of the president hung all over Baghdad. What is memorable is that the paintings were all done in deep reds and dark browns: later, I learned that Saadi had painted them with his own blood.

2

I WILL WAIT FOR YOU

If it takes forever I will wait for you
For a thousand summers I will wait for you

Jacques Demy

My father's name was Jaber Alsaadi. He was born in December 1938 in a small village near Nasiriyah where he grew up. Nasiriyah is about 360 kilometers (225 miles) southeast of Baghdad. The city is not far from the Arab Marshes, the Tigris-Euphrates wetlands that were, sadly, drained during and after the 1991 uprising. Prior to the oil boom of the 1970s, Iraq was a relatively poor country and, away from the capital, most people survived through subsistence farming and fishing. My grandfather supported his family by building boats; it was not a profitable trade, and my father's childhood was marked by desperate poverty.

Fortunately, Father was smart and he became the first person in his family to win a place at the university (in Iraq, university is free). He became one of the top students, and was awarded a scholarship to study in the USSR which, at that time, had a close relationship with Iraq and offered opportunities to its best and brightest.

My father studied in the Soviet Union through the 1960s, ultimately earning a Ph.D in Food Science. He spent several years working for the government of Syria, and was then asked by the Iraqi Minister of Industry to return to work for his native country. He was initially offered a consulting position but, through a combination of hard work and personal charm, he quickly rose through the ranks to become General Director, a level subordinate to only the minister and vice-minister. He was in charge of huge, complex government projects in which he would work with foreign experts, mostly from Eastern Europe, to build centralized factories producing nutritional staples like cooking oil, tomato paste and baby formula. He was involved in every aspect of construction, from initial planning, to production and distribution. He even got involved with packaging design and used my sister Tania's face for the infant formula and baby food labels.

My father's family was enormously proud of him, but his status and success also caused them to be suspicious of my mother. They thought she stole him away for his wealth, ignoring the fact that he spent a large percentage of his income on them. He bought his impoverished relatives clothes, cars, even houses, but nothing was ever enough and relations with them were always difficult.

Father was a complicated man. He was handsome, with fair skin, green eyes and a natural charm that gave him an edge in his personal and business dealings. Adding to his charm was a high level of self-confidence, and a talent for inspiring confidence in others. He was knowledgeable and ambitious, but often reckless in his pursuits. And he was driven by dual passions—for women and for wealth. He began to lead two lives, walking a tightrope between his public persona as a loyal government employee and a secret life he struggled to hide from his family, and from the authorities.

I knew my father was an important man. He spent most of his time at work, and he always wore a suit—my mother, who abhorred anything approaching bad taste, saw to it that his appearance was impeccable. I was quite afraid of him. He didn't beat us, but he had a temper and, when angered, would shout to the point where the room would shake. He was also distant, always keeping us at arms-length. I assume this was because he was raised that way; my paternal grandfather was the same. In fact, when Grandfather Alsaadi came to visit, he would never speak to us, or even look at us. All families have their own rhythm, and I never expected anything else.

As a handsome man with an important job, Father easily attracted women. He enjoyed their attention, and the illicit thrill of the extramarital affair. Even though the majority of Iraq's population was Muslim, it was a secular society and we did not have Sharia law (as Iran did after its 1979 revolution). The Ba'ath Party publicly denounced western nations as enemies of Iraq, while accepting French and American military supplies and weapons, and importing products and culture from Europe and North America. This relative openness made it easier for my father to spend a lot of time with other women; being a resourceful and determined man, he likely would have done what he pleased, regardless of the social climate.

I don't think Father felt particularly guilty about his lifestyle; there were certainly no qualms from a religious standpoint—my parents were not devout people. We were of the minority Mandaean faith which, though it is one of the world's oldest religions, has only about 70,000 remaining followers worldwide. The word Mandaean means 'knowledge' in Aramaic, which is the language spoken by the Mandaeans, who believe themselves to be descendants of Adam, and count Noah and John the Baptist among their prophets. Mandaeans are thought to be one of the few surviving Iraqi peoples whose culture dates back to the pre-Arab, pre-Islamic civilizations of Sumer and Babylon. However, there remains confusion as to the true origin of Mandaeism; some believe it is a post-Christian religion that originated with the Sabians, who are believed to belong to the prophet Noah. Others say that the Mandaeans are remnants of the Jewish tribes who remained in Babylonia after the other tribes left for Jerusalem (Mandaean teachings and rituals conflict with this thesis). Whatever their exact origin, the Mandaeans are profoundly fond of water and are often found living along river banks, where they practice baptism repeatedly in their ceremonies. Like most minorities in Iraq, they kept to themselves, traditionally working as artisans: goldsmiths, silversmiths and boat-makers, although later generations saw many of them become doctors, engineers and teachers. At one time, Muslims had seen them as impure and there had been discriminatory practices; for example, if a Mandaean had drunk from a glass, the glass would be broken. Under the Ba'ath Party, however, Mandaeans were protected and free to practice their religion.

Mandaeans can only marry within the faith, and divorce is forbidden. This made things complicated for my mother, Sawsan Saif. As a beautiful woman and an accomplished artist, she had many proposals, but she didn't want to marry anyone at all, until she met my father.

My mother had grown up in a prominent family that insisted that its children focus on the sciences, but her passion was the arts. After much cajoling, however, she was allowed to attend the highly-respected Baghdad Academy of Fine Arts, eventually graduating at the top of the class of 1966. She was then hired by Baghdad's Natural History Museum, where her job included replicating the natural habitats of various animals, and designing Iraqi stamp collections in themes relating to nature. That led to an invitation to submit designs for the national currency; her theme (eventually edged out by 'Arabian Horses') was the Birds of Iraq, and I think of that every time I look at Canadian currency. In 1980, she was hired as an artistic director by the Baghdad Convention Centre until she resigned in 1983 to focus on her family and art work.

Throughout her art career, my mother participated in a large number of exhibitions in Iraq and abroad. I have a vague recollection of attending a 1982 exhibition, in Casablanca, which was inaugurated by a daughter of the Moroccan king. As the story goes, we had to wait for this woman to arrive for the opening, and I was becoming restless. My mother told me that if I was patient, I would get to see a real princess. At four years old, I imagined a princess to be a Disney-like character with long blond hair, white skin and blue eyes. When she eventually showed up, this princess had dark skin and was quite old—I made a scene, shouting, "This ugly woman is no princess!"

My mother held her own private shows and, in 1972, had an art exhibition that, for some reason, was extended for one day. On that day, my father came to see her work. She didn't know it at the time, but Father's appearance was no coincidence. While he pretended that he had never heard of her, he knew a lot about her—the Mandaean community is small, and she was well-known.

My father had just returned from four years in Syria, and he had picked up the accent—it would have been like a North American returning from four years in England. This manner of speaking, in addition to his natural charm and good looks, captivated Mother. Plus, he was a cultured man in an important government position. She was hooked. They married in October 1972. My father did not want a big event and the ceremony was so modest, there is not a single photograph to mark the day. This presaged what was to come, as it was not long before the marriage deteriorated. Father continued to prioritize his own family and he was often absent, either at work or with other women.

My mother was aware of his affairs and fought to force him to change his behaviour. I remember hearing terrible arguments and, on more than one occasion, she called women to shame them. But, despite the deception and conflict, my mother never considered leaving my father. The divorce ban aside, she loved him with a devotion bordering on obsession. She was constantly seeking his love and devotion, and became prone to melodramatic attention-getting gestures. I remember once coming home to find her sprawled out on the floor, motionless. I didn't know if she was dead, or in a coma; she was fine—it was something staged for my father's benefit, to shock him into reacting. He did not. The psychological warfare failed to inspire him to devote more time and effort to his marriage. It was just the way things were; sometimes he would be at home with his family; more often, he was at work, with other women, or with his brothers, sisters and parents, to whom he remained very close.

■ ■ ■

Despite his senior government position, my father refused to join the Ba'ath party, and by the mid '70s, he had few illusions as to the true nature of the nation's ruling regime, which was becoming bloodier and more oppressive every year. Fearing the worst for the future of the country, he took the decision to get his family somewhere safe, and for that he took an enormous risk.

From his early years as General Director, he worked with foreign individuals and companies who were eager to gain a foothold in the Iraqi market. Under the Ba'ath party, Iraq was officially a planned economy, but capitalism was still healthy and the country was flooded with cash from the oil boom. As an official traveling throughout Europe on business for the Ministry of Industry, Father was in a unique position to offer guidance to those who wanted to do business inside Iraq. He had access to a depth of information about the Iraqi economy; he knew what the government was looking for, how to properly structure bids, and how to deal with the cumbersome bureaucracy. Leveraging his extensive knowledge, he signed consulting deals for his own account, earning him hard currency that he deposited abroad. When the time came to leave, it would be impossible to take money out of the country and the family would need cash. That made earning money outside of Iraq, and a foreign bank account, essential.

In many parts of the world, such consulting business by a civil servant was frowned upon due to the potential conflict of interest, but in Iraq it was punishable by death. Any unauthorized business dealings with outsiders was strictly illegal, even treasonous. Just having a foreign bank account, as my father had, was a capital offense.

Father was careful to keep all of this hidden but, in the end, he was exposed by politeness and gratitude. In 1980, one of his clients sent a letter to our home, thanking him for his help in his attempts to do business in Iraq. The letter was intercepted by the Secret Service. My father was arrested, accused of spying for foreign interests, and taken away.

■ ■ ■

The term 'Revolutionary Tribunal' has its origins in the French Revolution and the subsequent Reign of Terror, when political prisoners were tried by ad-hoc juries and often convicted with little or no evidence. In Iraq, under Ba'ath Party rule, the Revolutionary Tribunal acted as a court that carried out the will of the government, which was to identify and eliminate perceived enemies of the state. My father was brought before this kangaroo court to face charges of espionage and treason. The guilty verdict was a foregone conclusion; almost no one walked away from the tribunal. Given the seriousness of the charges, a guilty verdict meant only one thing: execution. And my mother was determined to stop it.

Despite his enormous wealth and power, Saddam Hussein fashioned himself a 'Man of the People'. As a gesture to his citizens, he instituted the 'Thursday Phone Call Program', through which any Iraqi was permitted to call the presidential palace and ask to speak with the president.

Deciding that a direct appeal would be her husband's best chance at survival, my mother called the number and was, to her surprise, connected to Saddam. She gave an impassioned summary of Father's arrest and detention, and Saddam granted her an audience.

As noted, my mother is a well-known artist. In the '70s, she was creating large, impressionistic oil paintings with a distinctly Middle Eastern, or even Babylonian, feel. When she went to the palace to meet with President Hussein, she presented him with one of her best paintings and a long letter, in which she made the case that her husband was a patriot and a loyal worker, not a traitor. Pleading with this all-powerful man, who had the discretion to either execute or release my father with a word, she told Saddam about the factories my father had built for Iraq, and how he was instrumental in creating the infrastructure that made it a strong, respected nation. Knowing that Saddam was dedicated to the idea of developing Iraq into a regional superpower, she explained that my father was a man who had given his sweat and blood for his country and his government: a smart, hard-working man whose skills and knowledge would be needed in the coming years. The charges, she said, were completely false—there had been a huge misunderstanding.

Saddam looked at my mother, and at the unread letter she had put on his desk. After a moment, he responded. Speaking in the deliberate and distinct accent native to his hometown of Tikrit north of Baghdad, he told her, "In this part of the world, even the rulers are not above justice. If a king makes a mistake, or betrays his people, we cut his head off." Sensing that her visit had been in vain, she reached for the letter on the president's desk. But, with a gesture, he stopped her hand.

My mother returned home with the standard gold-plated wristwatch the president gave to all his personal visitors, knowing that the chances of Saddam changing his mind were slim to none. Then, a few days later came the startling news: Saddam had read that impassioned letter and was allowing my father to speak to the Revolutionary Tribunal in his own defense. This was unheard of; people accused of crimes against the state were simply not allowed to speak, ever.

Given this one last lifeline, my father seized it with both hands. Or rather, with his voice. I have already said that he was gifted with personal charm; with the charisma and oratorical skills that served him throughout his career, he eloquently denied all of the charges against him, and demonstrated that he was a dedicated civil servant who had been wrongfully accused. The tribunal members, perhaps weighing the extraordinary fact that President Hussein had taken a personal interest in the case, decided to believe him. He was released.

My father had escaped the blade that had been hanging over his neck, thanks to my mother's efforts and his own talent for self-preservation. After just a few months in detention, he came home. He was even allowed to return to his job at the ministry; it was as if nothing had happened.

One might think that, after having narrowly escaped death, Father would have walked the straight and narrow for the rest of his life. But out of stubbornness, or a sense of individualism, or perhaps even a belief that he was somehow not subject to the regime's law, only a few years passed before he once again put himself in mortal peril.

■ ■ ■

By 1985, five years into the fighting, the war with Iran was having a drastic effect on Iraqi society. My father, who had always been secretly critical of the Hussein regime, became increasingly discontented with how the country was being run. As the conflict dragged on, more and more resources were devoted to the war; from his position in the Ministry of Industry, he saw essential public projects being canceled or abandoned, while the war brought more death and misery.

Frustrated by the government's singular obsession with the military, he was looking for a way into the private sector. He started meeting with an expatriate Syrian named Abu Rafi, who owned a restaurant in Baghdad. Father had family contacts that were looking to import gold into Iraq, and Abu Rafi offered to help. My father didn't care about the restrictions that made this sort of commerce highly risky, even though similar activities had recently nearly resulted in his execution.

At the same time, he was becoming more outspoken with his political opinions. He had long been criticizing Saddam at home and, quietly, with other men in the Mandaean community. We were careful to appear loyal and patriotic to outsiders. Like all Iraqi families, we complied with the unwritten rule that required Saddam's official portrait to be displayed in our home, and we patiently consumed the constant stream of government propaganda from the state-run media. But when TV reporters would make bold boasts predicting an imminent victory over Iran, or when government fabrications about the state of the economy would be reported as fact in the newspaper, my father would crack a joke or make a sarcastic comment. This was forbidden. Fear of the very real consequences of loose speech forced us to keep our mouths shut, and never betray evidence of critical thought. If you had opinions or beliefs that didn't come from the approved government script, you kept them to yourself. There were spies everywhere and we knew it.

My father's growing disaffection made him careless. On a number of occasions, he invited Abu Rafi to our home for dinner, and the talk would always turn to politics. My mother was uncomfortable with this as she was not sure that Abu Rafi could be trusted. She noticed, for instance, that while he brought gifts of alcohol to our home, he never touched a drop. Middle Eastern countries are full of men who don't drink alcohol, but Mother never saw this man as particularly religious and suspected he had ulterior motives. She was right. Abu Rafi was an informant. He remained sober at my family's table so he could better perform his duties of seeking out, and reporting on, anyone who displayed dissident behaviour or anti-Saddam sentiment.

Unaware that his would-be business partner was a government informant, my father freely expressed his view that the regime was steering Iraq in the wrong direction and that someone else should be in power. This sort of seditious talk was the highest crime imaginable, short of actually taking arms against the government, and his conversations with this undercover agent had immediate consequences for us all.

One night, not long after Father began socializing with Abu Rafi, they came for us. My mother was putting me to bed, and a man simply walked in to my room, waved a pistol at us and ordered us to the living room.

Then, from Tania's bedroom, we heard a scream of terror. On her bedroom wall, by the door, were two switches, one for the light, one for the fan. But the fan was broken; when it was turned on, it made a loud drumming noise. The man who invaded her room hit the fan switch first. Poor Tania was awakened by the sudden drumming, followed by the bright lights, which in turn illuminated an armed man standing over her. She awoke from a peaceful sleep to a nightmare.

In the living room, we were all made to sit silently on the couch. A dozen men with guns surrounded us. They had no badges or uniforms; they didn't need them. Their confidence and weapons marked them as members of the Mukhabarat, or the Iraqi Intelligence Service (IIS). They were Saddam's secret police and their authority was absolute. They could do whatever they pleased; as suspected traitors, we had no rights of any kind.

On the living room floor sat a collection of bags, filled with cash. The men stated that this was clear evidence that my father was engaged in criminal activities. I later learned that they had brought the cash with them, but they were not content with just planting evidence. They began searching the house, looking for anything that pointed to a conspiracy against Saddam or the Ba'ath Party. They opened every cabinet, emptied every drawer, poked in every nook and cranny in every room of the house, seeking anything that could be deemed incriminating. They even dumped out the contents of the refrigerator and freezer, tearing open every food package to see if it contained hidden illicit items. As the search stretched into the night, I lay my head down on my mother's lap, trying to sleep while having a surreal feeling of watching events from afar, as if I was watching a movie.

Anyone willing to search long enough will find things that look suspicious, especially when the term 'suspicious' covers as much as it did in Iraq at that time. As the IIS men found various items, they would bring them to us accusingly, waving them in our faces as clear examples of our disloyalty. My grandmother had a bundle of old newspapers, relics from Iraq's pre-revolutionary Imperial era, when the nation still had a king and royal family. To keep such things, the men claimed, we must be traitors. Mother had a briefcase that held American cash, the six thousand dollars that she had earned at the art show in Morocco. In the eyes of the investigators, this was proof that we were up to no good.

During this noisy and destructive search, the men were careful to confiscate anything that had any value: jewelry, cash, silverware. It either went into bags or into their pockets. They even emptied my piggy bank, taking the small collection of foreign coins and bills that my father had brought back from his business trips. Like locusts denuding a wheat field, the IIS men took every single item of worth from our house.

Ironically, the house had been built with various secret compartments, to hide valuables from burglars. We had a nook beneath a bookshelf; we even had a hollow door. Despite their thorough search, the Mukhabarat never found the compartments, but alas my parents never used them; probably due to simple negligence. With nothing hidden, everything was taken.

We were then led to waiting cars, with my father in the lead car. As we rode in terrified silence through the dark streets, we stopped every ten minutes or so; Father's fear was so intense, the driver had to constantly let him out to relieve his bladder. There were other stops too, as the police officers visited homes of people my father knew, rounding them up as witnesses to his activities, or as co-conspirators in his alleged crimes. Looking for enemies, the men were dragging a very wide net, and anyone who was in regular contact with him was automatically a suspect. To my knowledge, most were only interrogated and only one person, a woman, was jailed.

This silent, growing motorcade eventually arrived at an unmarked building in a part of the city far from our neighbourhood. We were locked inside a spare windowless room: four bare walls, a tile floor, a small desk. Father was taken to an adjacent room for questioning.

My mother, who was pregnant with Tamara, held on to us and was clearly very frightened, but this alone was not enough to convince Tania and I that the situation was grave. Our mother was a naturally anxious person, and we had seen her frightened many times, often in circumstances that turned out to be less than dire. It was my grandmother's reaction that told us we were in a very bad place. Bibi, as we called her, was a strong woman, but she was visibly shaken, and the look of fear in her eyes told us how serious our plight was. Despite this, I don't remember feeling hopeless or terrified; I certainly didn't think I was going to die. I remember feeling as if an invisible shield was protecting me. It may be that children feel somehow invincible, or it could be that my mind found a way to detach from the threat of the situation. I felt that the events of the evening would surely end as soon as I opened my eyes. Lost in such thoughts, I fell asleep on the floor, with Tania beside me.

The sound of shouting came through the walls from the next room. Mother could hear angry, forceful questions. The men were interrogating my father, demanding that he spill the details of some vast conspiracy against Iraq, and that he give up the names of his cohorts. It is possible that the shouting was meant for us to hear, to inspire Mother to break down and confess something. There is little doubt that it wasn't the last time my father was interrogated. Although he never spoke of it to me, I am certain that much harsher questioning went on later, far from the ears of witnesses.

Eventually, after sixteen hours in our gloomy cell, a man came in and told us we could leave. Father would have to stay for a few more hours, but we could see him for a quick good-bye.

I was seven years old, but I still knew my father would not be following us home later that night, or any night. In a totalitarian state, children become politically aware at an early age, and I knew a little of how things really worked. I was not naive enough to think Father would be let go with a fine and a stern warning. I didn't know why they arrested him, but I sensed it was serious. This added up to the realization that this might be the last chance to see him for a long, long time.

Yet when we were allowed to see him, I still asked him if he would be coming home with us. I already knew the answer, maybe I simply wanted to hear his voice, maybe it was my way of letting him know that I cared about him. He tried to reassure me, saying he would be home in a few hours—but I knew this would not be; the harsh truth was that this brief moment was the last I would spend with my father for a long time.

Many months later, the government got around to officially sentencing him. The prosecutors claimed to have tapes of him speaking against the president and conspiring against the government, and suggested that his plan to import gold was part of a grander plan to fund dissent against the regime. That was all that was needed to condemn him to twenty-five years in prison.

People who grow up in free and democratic societies find this hard to understand but, in Iraq in the 1980s, the entire legal system, from the beat cops to the high-court judges, was a political tool serving the interests of the president and his Ba'ath Party. Civilians had no power, no rights and nowhere to turn for justice. At the top, power was absolute; at the bottom, it was non-existent.

Father was gone from late 1985 to 1988. It was the hardest part of living through the war. My family had lost almost everything: all of our savings, most of our belongings, and my father's income. Worse, there was the basic problem of not having a father. He may have been often absent from the home, but he was still the centre of our family and he was missing during the bleakest and most dangerous years we were to face.

His confinement affected my mother more than any of us. It took all of her strength not to descend into depression and despair, and to keep doing her part to help the family survive. We were lucky to have support from friends and neighbours. People would come to visit and slip a few dinars into Tamara's crib, giving us what they could. I remember feeling embarrassed at the thought of surviving on handouts from strangers, but it was better than not surviving at all.

I missed my father and desperately wanted him back, but I was also ashamed by what had happened to him. I was too embarrassed to tell my friends and classmates the truth. It was obvious he was not around; he wasn't there for parents' days, or any of the other events where a father would traditionally stand by his son. How could I tell my friends he was in prison? It was a shameful thing to be unpatriotic, or anti-Saddam, but I couldn't lie about why he was imprisoned and have people think he was a common criminal. So when kids asked where he was, I said he was away on business. Some believed me, others probably did not.

This shame was balanced by the knowledge that my father was still alive. Some of my schoolmates were in the opposite situation: their fathers had died fighting in the war and were seen as heroes who had brought glory to their families. But what good is glory when you've lost a parent? I remember one boy whose father had been killed in the fighting and, as a reward, his mother received a new car. Many of us including me, were envious of that car. But I eventually understood that the price of the car was this boy's father life, and that nothing would bring back that husband and father. So while I was embarrassed, I was also thankful that, one day, Father might come back to us.

■ ■ ■

The months following my father's imprisonment were hellish. Mother was caring for Tamara and her art brought little income, our house had been confiscated and we were scheduled to be evicted. Without the help of my maternal grandmother, we would have starved. Bibi had a small inheritance from her husband and she used this money to keep us clothed and fed.

Bibi is Aziza AlBadi, a strong and fascinating woman. At the age of sixteen, she was pulled out of school and forced into a marriage with an army veteran, a colonel twenty years her senior. He ran his household like a military base, requiring his children to keep to an unbending schedule of eating and sleeping, and ruling his wife as he would a subordinate in the ranks. But Bibi was no shrinking violet. Sharp and resourceful, she was also politically wise. Ba'ath Party agents assassinated her brother in the 1960s because of his ties to the Communist Party, and that left her with a permanent mistrust of the government and a general political awareness that few Iraqis had. Each morning, she would turn on the radio and listen to the U.S. government's Voice of America. We would sit together and hear the 'real' news about the war with Iran, telling us the facts and offering analysis that Iraqi state media would never report.

She moved in with us in 1984, after her husband died of Alzheimer's disease. Prior to that, we spent a lot of time at her home, chasing the chickens around her yard and learning the secrets of growing vegetables. One of the most popular holidays in the Mandaean faith is Banja, a celebration honouring the day God created Heaven and Earth. The approach of Banja meant that there would be a sheep or two, and I remember caring for them before their eventual ceremonial sacrifice. Such contradictions did not faze Bibi; she was a woman who 'got on with things'. She did not resent her forced marriage, or her husband's harsh treatment. She grew to love and respect him, and remained loyal to him after his death. In fact, she wore the black garb of mourning for an entire decade.

This is a woman who, on the day of Father's arrest and while being held for interrogation by the Mukhabarat, was bold enough to ask for her confiscated jewelry. Amazingly, the agents returned most of it. And when we returned to our ransacked house, she bought new furniture and covered the monthly expenses. She also became a replacement parent to my sisters and me, and provided much-needed emotional support for my devastated mother.

■ ■ ■

In the late summer of 1986, we were finally allowed to visit my father at Abu Ghraib, the infamous prison west of Baghdad. It was almost as hard to find transportation to the prison as it had been to secure permission for the visit. My mother didn't drive; my father's family had a car, but they were unreliable and rarely willing to help us, or even spend time with us. In fact, they had already been to see him and had not bothered to tell us. Still, after much begging and cajoling, one of my aunts agreed to give us a ride to the prison. So one steamy summer day found me packed into my aunt's car with my mother and two sisters. Even with the windows down, we were all sweating and suffering, but our spirits were high because we were going to see our father.

Abu Ghraib is a vast, sprawling complex. Built by British contractors in the 1960s, the forbidding, fortress-like compound was more than just a jail. It was a black hole of terror into which Saddam Hussein's political enemies disappeared to be tortured, starved and/or murdered. In Iraq in the 1980s, the prison was something people whispered about, as if they were talking about hell itself. For the government, that fear was an effective tool; the threat was 'stay in line and do not challenge us or you know where you will end up'.

My aunt parked the car on the outskirts of the complex and we made our way past the first checkpoint. We then had to walk for another twenty minutes to reach the building where my father was being held. Dozens of people walked with us, some wearing suits or western-style clothing, others in traditional Arab attire. Women young and old, some cloaked in the traditional abaya, carried food for their imprisoned husbands, fathers, sons or brothers. Others brought bags of necessities like soap, toothpaste and cigarettes, knowing that prisoners could use these items, or trade them for what they needed to survive.

The room where the prisoners slept was a single enormous space, like a warehouse, filled with row upon row of utilitarian steel bunk beds, perhaps a hundred or more, with my father's bunk somewhere near the middle. When we found him, he gave us warm hugs and took my baby sister Tamara in his arms for the first time. He looked thin and tired and ten years older. I later learned that all prisoners were required to give blood—more than a litre every two months, to supply the soldiers fighting in the war. That, combined with scarce and awful food, sub-standard sanitation, and the stress of living in confinement, resulted in a prison full of malnourished, weak and unhealthy men.

Outside my father's building was a concrete courtyard. It was open to the sky, except that there were large, ragged squares of fabric stretched between the high walls to provide shade, and the result was a giant tent. On the ground, there was a mass of dusty rugs carpets scattered about for people to rest on. My father sat down on one of these rugs and took me into his lap.

I recall vividly what happened next. I had a piece of skin peeling from the tender flesh around my fingernails—just a loose cuticle, which a child might absentmindedly play with but mostly leave alone because of the stinging pain. Without warning, my father reached down, grabbed this flap of skin and pulled it off, like he was ripping off a bandage. I don't know why he did this, but the shock and pain were nearly unbearable and I felt the tears spring instantly to my eyes. I bit my tongue and forced myself not to cry; I didn't want to upset him or spoil our time together.

My father then pointed to a nearby building, explaining that it was where the prison housed those who were scheduled for execution. Most of them were Shia Muslims accused of being allies of Iran. The Ba'ath Party banned all political parties, but the Shia Al-Dawa party was accused of plotting the 1982 attempt to assassinate Saddam. I listened quietly as my father explained that, every Wednesday, guards would circulate among the prisoners and, seemingly at random, choose the ones who would die. The entire prison population would remain silent on this day, watching what they called 'The Harvesting'.

Eventually, we said our tearful goodbyes and made the long, hot walk back to the car. We walked in silence, like shell-shocked soldiers. We didn't talk much on the drive home either. There just wasn't much to say.

Father spent a total of two and a half years away from us, most of it in Abu Ghraib. When he was finally released in mid-1988, it was, as before, thanks to my mother.

Mother did not talk much about our father while he was in prison, but I know that she never stopped thinking about him, and about getting him back. Despite her nervous anxiety and fearful nature, she was a dreamer and an optimist, and once she'd set her mind on something, she was determined and persistent.

My mother had used a direct appeal to Saddam Hussein to have my father released after his first arrest, and she opted to try the same tactic.

This time, she wanted me to call the palace. I begged her not to make me do it, but she was convinced that a young boy stood a better chance of being connected. Hesitant and embarrassed, I dialed the number and asked to speak with 'Uncle Saddam'. However, unbeknownst to us, the government had long since ended the 'Thursday Phone Call Program', and the number now put us in touch with an anonymous government employee in some unknown department who was utterly mystified by a little boy's request to speak to the supreme leader of Iraq.

Mother was undeterred. If she could not reach the president by phone, she would find another way. As she had in 1980, she decided to use her natural artistic talent to get a foot in the palace door. This time, she would make her offering coincide with the president's birthday, a day of celebration when many Iraqis sent their leader gifts. Saddam was said to be in a good mood around his birthday—more approachable and generous.

She knew that if she was going to make an impression, her gift to the dictator would have to stand out among all the other presents he would receive. She would have to paint something especially for Saddam, and it would have to be spectacular. She chose a large canvas, took out her paints and brushes, and set to work on her plan to once again spring her husband from prison.

The struggle between the Israelis and the Palestinians was always a subject of great concern to Saddam. His frustration deepened after Israel bombed an Iraqi nuclear plant in 1981, and 1987 was the year of the Palestinian Intifada against Israel. With this in mind, Mother decided that the theme of her painting would be the suffering of Palestinian children under the Israeli occupation. She painted a tragic, haunting image of a young naked Palestinian girl, viewed from behind, wearing only the traditional Middle Eastern headdress called a keffiyeh, and looking out at the smoking remains of a burning, utterly destroyed city.

Mother felt that this subject would convey the proper political message and appeal to Saddam's sympathy, while setting her apart from the opportunists who sought favour by glorifying his bloody regime with grandiose presidential portraits. I recall a neighbour joking that the painting might compel Saddam to declare war on Israel; three years later, Saddam did attack Israel, launching SCUD missiles in a desperate attempt to rally the Arab and Muslim world around him as he was being driven out of Kuwait during the 1991 Gulf War. Mother's painting had nothing to do with that, but it accomplished its goal: it got his attention and gained her an audience.

Just as she had done seven years earlier, my mother stood before Saddam Hussein and pleaded for her husband's release. Saddam had doubtless met with thousands of similarly desperate people and had no recollection of their previous meeting; he did not remember her or my father. Still, he listened politely as my mother argued my father's case, then he picked up his phone and asked an aide to bring him Father's file. Then, telling her that he did not like to see tears on the faces of Iraqi women, he again took pity. Once again, my mother left with a gold-plated watch with Saddam's picture on its face. Then, nothing.

Six months later, in the spring of 1988, the phone rang. It was the director of Abu Ghraib, who told Mother that, on the following Tuesday, her husband would be having lunch at home with his family. It was his melodramatic way of informing her that Father was being freed. All at once, we were stunned, relieved and elated. My mother and grandmother immediately enlisted the whole neighbourhood to prepare a feast, and the party was a joyous day for us all. Naturally, the happiest person was my father; from a system that offers few second chances, he had secured an amazing third chance.

Prison steals more than time, and takes from everyone. Tamara, who was born while Father was in captivity, had no idea who he was and, for some time, called him 'Uncle'. And my relationship with my father had changed. He was more distant and uncommunicative than ever, and what little warmth there had been between us was extinguished. But prison had not broken him. He was weaker and older, but still energetic. This time, he did not return to the Ministry of Industry—he started an import/export business. But he did return to his old habits of spending a great deal of time away from his family, and seeing other women.

My father's feelings towards my mother were more complicated than ever. Instead of love and gratitude, he felt great resentment. He was someone who had always controlled his own destiny, yet his wife had now twice saved his life. It was a debt he could never possibly repay, and the issue always remained 'the elephant in the room'. He could not talk about it, and he could not forget it.

3

MONEY

Money, money makes the world go round
Money, money'll make you change your sound

Jesca Hoop

On August 8, 1988, just a few months after Father's release, the Iran–Iraq War ended. The United Nations Resolution 598 ended all combat in what had become the longest war of the 20th century, and one of the most destructive wars ever fought between two developing nations.

All Iraqis hoped that peace would bring lasting change and prosperity. The national economy, decimated by nearly a decade of war, had nowhere to go but up and everyone wanted to get back to business. That included me—I was just ten when the war ended, but I was already developing a keen interest in earning money.

I had started my first 'business' when I was seven. The only businessmen I knew were the local shop-owners, and I knew that a man could make money by having a storefront and selling groceries, or hardware items, or clothing. So I needed a shop, and something to sell. I would rummage around inside the storage room of our house, looking for anything interesting or slightly valuable. I would then set up a 'shop' in the living room and invite my only customer, my mother, to come and buy my wares. She indulged me by giving me a few coins for items that already belonged to her. It wasn't brilliant, but it was a start.

My next attempt at commerce was a little more sophisticated and involved actual sales. When he was released from prison, Father started an import-export business through which he traded a wide variety of products. He received boxes of free samples, and I was allowed to shop them around the neighbourhood, selling things like cleaning supplies and bug spray to parents who indulged me because I went to school with their children. It certainly helped my bottom line that the profit margin on a free sample was always 100%.

Then I realized that I was needlessly limiting myself by sticking to a residential customer base. I started selling to the people who I thought of as 'real businessmen', the local shop-owners. When I wasn't in school, I would visit the small grocery stores closest to my house, presenting the shopkeepers with the items I had for sale—perhaps ten cans of shoe polish, or a dozen bottles of window cleaner. Often they would buy one or two items, sometimes they would not. Yet there was no end to the boxes Father brought home from companies and merchants eager to do business in Baghdad. The samples were piling up and I had to up my game.

I widened my circle of potential customers, venturing beyond my immediate neighbourhood and into the surrounding streets. Unable to carry much on my own, I recruited friends as a sales force, paying them commission on whatever they sold. The system worked well, and my salesmen were able to establish and maintain steady relationships with a number of shop-owners in our section of the city. After about two months of steady work, my cut of the profits came to about 110 dinars; the equivalent of one month's salary for most government employees. Given that my father had earned 320 dinars as Director General of the Ministry of Industry, this was not too shabby for a ten-year-old.

Sadly, I had little time to enjoy my success. The eviction notice that had been hanging over our heads was carried out. We moved to a new neighbourhood and I lost my network of salesmen and customers. But I adapted, and quickly hit on a new business venture.

By the summer of 1990, when I was twelve, the home computer revolution had arrived. The war with Iran had been over for two years and the economy was much stronger. People were hungry for all kinds of consumer electronics. Basic computer systems, similar to the Commodore computers sold in other countries, were the norm, with software sold on 3.5-inch floppy disks. We had one of these systems in our new home, which was located near a bustling commercial artery called 14 Ramadan Street, where there were several computer stores. I was a confident, good-looking kid with the ability to charm and impress my elders, and I took to chatting with the shop owners about the latest products and trends. One of these guys took a liking to me, and decided to let me have a stack of disks with about one hundred popular games on them. I thanked him for the generous gift and walked out of the store, knowing I was back in business.

At home, I copied the games onto blank disks, which I then peddled to other computer shops around the neighbourhood, telling them that I was selling on behalf of an older cousin so they wouldn't squeeze me on the price. I was now a software distributor, charging one or two dinars for bootlegged computer games. I made 150 dinars in the first month, and once again, was able to expand my business into new territory.

I told one of my regular customers that my family was about to embark on a trip around Europe, on a vacation we had always dreamed of but had been unable to take during the long war. My customer, knowing that foreign items always brought premium prices, suggested that I take my profits, load up on new games and other software while in Europe, and bring the disks back to Baghdad to sell. The thought thrilled me. I would have my own import/export business, like my father, but in the cutting-edge business of personal computing. I knew I could easily double or triple my investment, and from there, the sky would be the limit.

We left for our European tour on July 2, 1990. On the way to the airport, we were ecstatic. Traveling to Europe was something magical and it had been years since we had been anywhere. Tania and I had dreamt of this day for what seemed an eternity: now it was becoming a reality. The highway taking us to the airport was almost empty and the taxi was speeding. We passed a bronze statue of a man wearing feathered wings, like a flying angel; this was Abbas Ibn Firnas, the Andalusian Icarus who made wings of feathers and tried to fly. As the car raced on, I felt just like Ibn Firnas, ready to don my wings and take off.

We were meant to fly to Vienna, but when we arrived at the airport, our flight was overbooked. We found an alternative flight—to Istanbul, and that became our first stop out. Istanbul was technically in Europe, and a beautiful bustling city, but it was not the real thing—we were eager to visit Vienna, Paris and London. We chose to make the best of it and checked into a modest hotel with very basic furniture and no TV. I remember the first morning in the breakfast room, when the waiter spilled a jug of milk on me. The poor guy was extremely panicked and he rushed me to the washroom to clean me up. I spoke very little English at the time, but I remember telling him, "It's okay, it's okay...".

We spent a week touring the exotic city. I was very impressed by Hagia Sophia, the former orthodox basilica that had been converted into a mosque after the Ottomans conquered Constantinople in the 15th century. I had seen many mosques in Baghdad, but a hybrid of a mosque and a church was a strange sight; it was as if two structures from two dimensions had merged into one. I also distinctly remember crossing the Bosphorus Bridge from the European side of Istanbul to the Asian side, with the massive ships crossing the river, the deep blue sea below and the strong wind blowing around us.

Our next stop was Vienna, where my priority was to visit the renowned Sacher Hotel. My father used to return from European trips with a classic wooden box containing the famous Sachertorte, a mouth-watering combination of chocolate cake and apricot jam. I was ecstatic to be able to go to its 'home'. To enter the grand hotel, sit below the great crystal chandeliers and savour the best confection in the world was a real thrill. The sensation was one of pure joy and I will never forget it.

On August 2, one month after we had left Baghdad, we were still seeing the galleries and museums of Vienna when our vacation ended. The Iraqi army invaded the neighbouring nation of Kuwait, an action that would eventually lead to the Gulf War. All of a sudden, we were back in war mode. The newspapers carried pictures of Iraqi tanks, planes and missiles; Saddam appeared on television. War had followed us to Europe.

■ ■ ■

By September 1990, there had not yet been an American and coalition military response to the Iraqi invasion of Kuwait, but my parents knew it was coming. Unlike many Iraqis, who lived in denial and somehow still trusted their government, my parents were under no illusions. The United States was not sending all those troops, planes and ships to simply be a 'Desert Shield' against further Iraqi territorial claims. They were going to attack Iraq.

My parents could not bear to live through another war. They resolved to settle in France, an easy choice given that my father had many contacts there, my mother adored the country and Paris had an Iraqi school. We landed at Charles De Gaulle Airport on September 3 and found that, thanks to Saddam's invasion of Kuwait, Iraqis were persona non grata. Even though we had the right visas, we were detained for six hours before being allowed to leave the airport. My first act in

France was to overlook a metal bar near the airport gate and hit my head so hard that my head was spinning for the entire ninety-minute drive to the hotel.

In the first few days of our stay, Father was busy securing our residency, so the rest of us toured the Eiffel tower, the natural history museum, the Louvre and other attractions. But our hearts weren't in it; we were more concerned with our reality, which was that we were now stranded in a strange country and unsure about our fate, and the fate of friends and family back home.

My grandmother, who was travelling with us, was not sure whether she wanted to return to Iraq. She had learned that her son, my uncle Lamie, had managed to get the last plane out of Kuwait City and had made it to Sweden. She thought she might want to immigrate to Sweden as well, but said that if she did want to return to Iraq, she would need dinars. Luckily, I had brought the 200 dinars I had earned through my software sales with me and I decided to give it to her. She then left for Sweden where her daughter-in-law, a troubled woman who never cared for my grandmother, went through her purse and stole the dinars. Bibi stayed in Sweden and didn't need the money—but that was my savings. Over the course of my life, I have found that there are many ways to lose all the money you have. But having it snatched out of my grandmother's purse by a disturbed woman a thousand miles away is certainly the strangest way it has ever happened to me.

■ ■ ■

Through an acquaintance, my father found an apartment in the 16th district, across from the Radio France building. It was a nice little first-floor apartment with wooden floors and a balcony overlooking a small garden. School started a few weeks later, my sister and I started taking the bus every morning and, just like that, we had to start a new life, make new friends and accept that our European vacation had been transformed into exile.

On January 17, 1991, we watched CNN in silence, as hell was unleashed on Baghdad and its sky blazed with missiles and anti-aircraft fire. I felt anger, fear and hopelessness as my hometown burned in front of my eyes. Those feelings, however, were mixed with a sense of relief that we weren't there, and a sense of guilt for not being there for my friends, neighbours and loved ones.

Even though my father had always planned that we would leave Iraq, the suddenness and uncertainty of the situation made him refer to it as a 'temporary holding pattern'. When the scope of the Gulf War's destruction became clear, though, we knew there was no going back. At the start of the coalition's initial aerial bombing campaign, U.S. Secretary of State James Baker announced to the world that America would "send Iraq back to the Middle Ages", and this is essentially what the war did. The bombing, and the subsequent years of sanctions, destroyed Iraq's economy, obliterated the infrastructure and reduced the populace to beggars. Without food and clean water, starvation and disease were rampant. Much of the Baghdad I had known as a child was gone, reduced to rubble and ash.

While people around the world were happy to see the tyrant Saddam defeated, it was the ordinary citizens of Iraq, including millions of children, who suffered. The American-led coalition's missiles did in a few weeks what Iran was unable to do in eight years.

This was devastating to me. I wanted to go back to Iraq. To my friends, my business, my school—I wanted to resume my life. (Eventually, all of our possessions were seized by my father's family, who despised us for escaping the war. Throughout the 1990s, to spite us, my aunt and cousins sent us pictures of themselves wearing our clothes and living in our house.)

Still, we were lucky. Father's consulting work may nearly have cost him his life, but now it paid off. He had many European contacts—and he had that foreign bank account. His consultancy earnings had not been touched for nearly twenty years and the magic of compound interest transformed his savings into a sizable nest egg that gave us the means to stay in Europe. That is what entrenched in my mind the importance of having money. It also made crystal clear the relationship between risk and return.

■ ■ ■

I did not enjoy living in France. I did not fit in. There was a good deal of mistrust between French citizens and the millions of North Africans and Arabs living in France. As I was from Iraq, I was automatically classified as 'Arab' and that subjected me to discrimination, even though Iraqis had little in common with North African Arabs. As a non-Muslim (and, by that time, an atheist) I was even further alienated from the Arab community, but the French saw me as one of 'them'.

In the early '90s, Parisians were in the grip of a nationalistic wave, one that was exacerbated by a deteriorating economy and was frequently manifest as racism, hostility and violence. Arabs, tired of being spat on and denigrated, often responded in kind. One of the harshest consequences was a three-pronged anti-immigration program put forward by right-wing Interior Minister Charles Pasqua and launched under the popular slogan 'Immigration Zéro'. This policy had a devastating effect on refugees (which is what we really were). Our residency permits had to be renewed every three months, and Immigration Zéro made it a hellish ordeal that included verbal abuse and degrading treatment at the French immigration office. (In 2004, the Iraqi daily Arabic newspaper al Mada published a memorable list of people who allegedly received corruption money from Saddam's government during the course of the infamous UN Oil-for-Food Program. Pasqua's name appeared on that list; after several years of investigations he was cleared of the charges in July 2013).

This boldly drawn racial divide left me with an identity crisis. I looked European, yet I spoke Arabic. In Baghdad, I was part of a minority, but at least there were a few thousand of us; in Paris, I seemed to be a minority of one. I have always been a bit of a perfectionist and I was reluctant to speak French conversationally without first being fluent. I hated the idea of making mistakes in my speech. So when I was not with Arabic-speaking people, I spent most of my time with Tania, or alone. This, of course, further alienated me from many potential friends. I should have put more effort into improving my French and finding ways to integrate into Parisian life.

Part of my reluctance stemmed from the fact that our family's relocation to France had been forced and I resented being there. If going back to Baghdad was not an option, I wanted my parents to move us to London; in Iraq, English is taught from the fifth grade and I knew enough that I wouldn't have to start from scratch. Also, Iraq was an ex-British colony and we were more familiar with British culture. But London was not an option: the Iraqi school in London only went to the tenth grade, so Tania, who was about to start the eleventh grade, would have been excluded.

Why are there Iraqi schools in Europe? This was part of the Ba'ath Party's strategy; it established Iraqi schools in most of the world's capitals as a way of spreading its ideology. It was an expensive endeavour, but it was important for the regime because it indoctrinated Arabic-speaking people at an early age.

My isolation in France increased my focus on Iraq. After the Gulf War ended, the sanctions had the effect of killing more people than the war itself, through lack of food, medicine and the parts and equipment required to repair infrastructure. I became political in the way only angry young people can. I was vocal about my opposition to the sanctions, and I wore custom t-shirts with the Iraqi flag and anti-sanctions statements. I also built and maintained an information website that detailed the suffering of the Iraqi people.

My frustration increased with the pace of U.S. cruise missile strikes (one of which killed my mother's best friend and her husband, and blinded her daughter). Then there were statements by American officials, such as the following, which I watched on *60 Minutes* in May of 1996:

Interviewer Lesley Stahl on U.S. sanctions against Iraq: "We have heard that a half million children have died. I mean, that's more children than died in Hiroshima. And, you know, is the price worth it?"

Secretary of State Madeleine Albright: "I think this is a hard choice, but the price—**we think the price is worth it**."

To me, the sanctions were war crimes. The Iraqi people suffered a modern-day holocaust for deeds committed by their leader—a man who had been backed by the West, including the United States, throughout the 1980s. In my desperation, I wrote letters to President Clinton and French President Jacques Chirac, asking them to stop punishing the Iraqi people, lift the economic sanctions and allow Iraq to rebuild.

It was around that time that I began to seriously question the meaning of life. Somewhere along the line, I had lost my belief in God and religion. I started to see life as a meaningless endeavour, and as more of a burden than a gift. I understood that people create narratives that give their lives meaning, but 'meaning' is subjective and there is no universal definition of truth. Truth is subject to interpretation and manipulation, consciously or otherwise. All of the senseless violence and injustice I had witnessed haunted me, and reminded me that the universe is a desolate and harsh place, and that human civilization could end as easily as it started if a stray asteroid came our way.

As I questioned the purpose of human existence, I came across the writing of the late astrophysicist Carl Sagan, and the photograph of Earth taken by the space probe Voyager, at Sagan's request. In this fascinating picture, taken at a distance of four billion miles, Earth appears as a tiny fraction of a pixel against the vast background of space, and in his book *Pale Blue Dot*, Sagan reflects:

> "...The Earth is a very small stage in a vast cosmic arena. Think of the rivers of blood spilled by all those generals and emperors so that in glory and triumph they could become the momentary masters of a fraction of a dot. Think of the endless cruelties visited by the inhabitants of one corner of this pixel on the scarcely distinguishable inhabitants of some other corner. How frequent their misunderstandings, how eager they are to kill one another, how fervent their hatreds. Our posturing, our imagined self-importance, the delusion that we have some privileged position in the universe, are challenged by this point of pale light. Our planet is a lonely speck in the great enveloping cosmic dark. In our obscurity—in all this vastness—there is no hint that help will come from elsewhere to save us from ourselves..."

Sagan's words continue to ring true to me and I often think of the picture of that pale blue dot when I observe life around me and wonder if my life will ever have meaning.

Despite my focus on Iraq, by age fifteen, I was steadily losing my sense of identity. I figured I could not stay in the Iraqi school in France, where I was unhappy and disconnected from my classmates. I also had a serious conflict with my math teacher, whose computations I had dared to correct. He was not the sort of man to accept being questioned, and he disliked me intensely. He was also, like many other people at the school, suspicious of my father. Even though it was in Paris, the school was sponsored and maintained by the Iraqi government, and still controlled by Saddam and the Ba'ath Party. My father had twice been arrested, and released, by the regime and was now living a relatively successful life in a western country. The ex-patriot Iraqi community didn't know where his allegiances lay and they were cautious about interacting with him. This distrust and fear naturally affected how the teachers and administrators viewed our whole family, and that added to my discomfort.

Most importantly, I wanted to move on. But to go forward with the next phase of my life, I would have to perfect my English. English was the language of business and trade, and of the nascent Internet. So, in the ninth grade, I transferred to the International School of Paris, where the teachers and students spoke only English. That's when I realized how limited my English education had been. I was lost. I did not have the words to participate in class and the resultant dramatic drop from Ideal Student to Bottom of the Class was very painful. Luckily, I was able to enroll back in the Iraqi school, but this time I joined the distance-learning program, which allowed me to study at home and only appear at the school for exams. At the same time, I attended a special intensive English program offered at an American fashion school in the city.

I now had more free time and spent some of it getting to know Paris a little better. I rode the Metro, getting off at random stops and walking the neighbourhoods. I climbed the majestic Eiffel tower and walked the banks of the Seine. I discovered the post-modern art museum Palais de Tokyo, which would become a recurring destination. And I relished trips to the supermarket. After years of war, we had mostly empty shelves back home; in Paris, the market was full of everything my heart desired, particularly the famous French cakes, pastries and chocolate.

I also started to enjoy meeting different types of people. For example, Tania and I were sitting in McDonald's one day when a man approached us. He had heard us talking and confirmed that we were from Iraq. Then, with tears in his eyes, he explained that he too was Iraqi but, in the 1940s, his family was expelled—along with the rest of the nation's Jews, in response to the creation of Israel. He sat and talked with us for some time, sharing stories and asking questions about our home. He was the first Israeli person I had ever met; that would not have been possible in Iraq.

■ ■ ■

In order to stay in France, we had to be seen to be contributing to the economy. My father attempted to resume his import/export business by partnering with an old business acquaintance, but the war and the sanctions severely limited his ability to export merchandise to Iraq. He briefly worked with another businessman who needed capital to expand a detergent distribution business, but this venture also failed.

In 1992, Father met a fellow Iraqi who owned a small, shabby hotel in the 15th district. They struck a deal: Father agreed to buy a fifty percent stake in the hotel, and to use his capital to repair and improve the property—an investment that required all the money he had. Eighteen months later, the partner wanted out. My father needed the hotel to keep our visas and was forced to buy the man's share. He borrowed heavily, at 11% interest, to become the sole owner of a hotel worth $2 million.

It was readily apparent that he had no idea what he was doing. He was an expert in food manufacturing—he didn't know anything about running a boutique hotel. He began to sink into debt and his solution was to cut corners to lower expenses. He failed to make necessary upgrades in areas such as security and fire safety and he started deferring taxes in questionable ways in order to maintain working capital. He survived, but just barely.

By age sixteen, I was helping out, putting in shifts at reception and performing other tasks. But my French was not good, and I found that

I was not well-suited for customer service, chasing after guests to pay their bills, and dealing with requests and complaints. I felt frustrated and resentful.

The pressure of the hotel business also took a heavy toll on my parents' relationship. It was not a healthy relationship to start with, but the stress of running a business that requires constant attention wore down my father. His exhaustion was reflected in an ever-boiling temper. Once, after a particularly violent fight with my mother, he kicked us all out of the house and a family friend had to intervene to get us back home. This sort of thing became characteristic of our life in Paris; Father often gave the impression that he could do without us. It was a cold and disturbing feeling to have a father who alternated between wanting to provide and care for us, and a furious man who was ready to discard us.

■ ■ ■

Through all of this, I had not lost my financial and business ambitions. Forces beyond my control had torpedoed my first two attempts at starting businesses. Then, one night, we went to a dinner party at the home of a Lebanese man with whom my father was doing business. I was sitting quietly as the adults talked when, amidst the chatter, I heard someone say that the host had "lost his entire fortune in the stock market". The words rang loud in my ears. A 'fortune'? The 'stock market'? I remember the rush of excitement I felt at being somehow in the domain of high finance, even if it was just a suggestion in the air. It was the first time I recall feeling the 'pull' that would draw me ever closer to the world of finance. I had discovered The Stock Market, a place where vast fortunes were made. This discovery would define the rest of my life.

Shortly after that dinner, I started watching the stock market—literally. Every day after school, I would sit and watch the tickers on the European Business Network. One day in 1995, when I was 17, I concluded that watching the market was not enough and resolved to buy my first stock. Euro Disney had gone public few years earlier, at 21 francs per share. At the time I decided to buy it, it was trading around 10 francs and I thought that was a steal. I put on my best clothes and headed to my bank.

As I waited for the account manager, I felt like a million dollars. Here I was just minutes from transacting on the stock market; finally I wasn't just watching the action, I was joining it. The account manager was an old man, a caricature of the typical Frenchman with curly hair, a thin moustache and a red nose from drinking too much wine. We went into his office, I told him I wanted to buy 10,000 francs ($1500) worth of Euro Disney stock and three days later, I received a letter confirming that my order had been executed at 10.8 francs. It had taken all of my savings, but I was the proud owner of 920 Euro Disney shares.

The stock dropped. Every day, the ticker on my television screen brought me bad news about my investment. I quickly realized that what I had thought was a smart, prudent choice was actually a dog, and that my first trade was going to be a swift and harsh lesson rather than an easy profit. Unwilling to sell at a loss, and left with no more cash to invest, I made no more trades for two years, partly because I felt burned; mostly because I was broke.

4

MAGIC CARPET RIDE

Why don't you tell your dreams to me
Fantasy will set you free

Steppenwolf

By the time I was ready for university, my English was good enough that I was able to start at Schiller International University, which is one of the two American universities in Paris. After one year there, I opted to transfer to Saint Mary's University in Halifax, Nova Scotia. I was eager to leave France and Schiller did not offer a finance program. Canada seemed like the right choice and I wanted to live in a smaller city. I knew nothing of Halifax, other than that a G-7 meeting had been held there two years before, which made it seem important. Also, I had read that Canada had great universities and that they were much less expensive than American colleges. Saint Mary's had a good reputation for business education, and I was glad to be accepted.

I arrived in Halifax in August 1997. The city was nice, a beautiful environment with vast green spaces. But it was the first time I had left my family, and I felt lonely, isolated and scared. I was nineteen and knew only one person—my good friend Aristotle, who also came from

Paris to attend university. Having Ari there softened the blow of separation somewhat yet, at first, there was an intense, hollow feeling of homesickness and at least once, I was forced to hide tears from my new classmates.

In many Middle Eastern cultures, the mother rules the roost. The atmosphere within the home is protective and nurturing in a way that, to westerners, would seem restrictive or even smothering. There is no desire, as there is in North America, to kick the kids out of the nest and let them fly solo. In fact, children are usually expected to remain with their parents into early adulthood, sometimes even until marriage. This was certainly the case in my family. While my Canadian and American classmates came to university as carefree and confident individuals, my own transition from 'son' to 'independent student' took a little more time and effort. My new friends were eager to get away from their families and experience freedom, but I found independence daunting. Even something as simple as cooking presented a challenge. Life under my parents' roof had left me spoiled and unprepared for college life.

That is why my years in Halifax were so important. The sudden change in surroundings and lifestyle forced me to grow more independent, to become a true individual, disconnected from the collective of my family. I also started to develop a deep appreciation for the country and its people; I felt Canada could be my home.

Halifax is a student town, with two big universities: Dalhousie, which is more science-oriented and has a well-known law school, and Saint Mary's, which is more focused on the social sciences. Halifax, like most of Canada, is blessed with beautiful nature and is often called 'The City of Trees', although its oceanfront position makes for a lot of wind and winters are especially severe. When I arrived, the people were very welcoming and friendly, and staying in the university dorm immersed me in Canadian and Nova Scotia culture. This is where I experienced my first Thanksgiving dinner, learned words like 'pop', 'Loonie',

'Canuck' and 'eh', watched my first hockey and football games, ate my first Donair, drank Keith's beer, tasted maple syrup, and learned of the Acadians. It was all new to me, but I was fascinated with the country, and still am.

When I was living and studying in Halifax, my financial circumstances were very different. My father had given me $50,000 to cover tuition and living expenses for the three years it would take to finish my education in Canada. I concluded, however, that the money offered a fantastic opportunity to get back into the stock market—a market that was on the verge of something big.

I sensed that the Internet was transforming the world, and I believed that the companies that were building the hardware, software and culture of the Internet and World Wide Web held the possibility for enormous growth. In October 1997, I opened a trial account with E-Trade, and earned an impressive 20% return on my investment in my first month of trading Internet stocks. Excited and emboldened by this initial success, I took half of my money, $25,000, and went full-force into the market.

I knew that many people were now making a living as 'day traders', but I chose a slightly different path by investing as a 'swing trader', meaning that I held onto my shares for a few days, weeks or even months before selling. I did not have much experience and wasn't terribly smart about many of my trades. My prime focus was to find promising, growing companies with a connection to emerging technology or the Web, such as the early pre-Google search engine companies like Lycos, Infoseek and Excite. (I was briefly interested in investing in crude oil futures when oil prices sunk under $10.00 a barrel in the late '90s, but Exchange-Traded Funds, or ETFs, did not yet exist. The process of buying oil futures was also more complicated than trading stocks online, so I abandoned the idea and focused exclusively on technology stocks.)

Between December 1997 and October 1999, I led a dual life. Part of the day, I was a student, attending classes, completing papers and taking exams. The rest of the time, I was a stock market investor, researching companies, identifying opportunities and making trades. Of course, I also went out for beers with my friends and took in the occasional movie. But these ordinary pursuits didn't provide the thrill that came from getting into an IPO, buying $10,000 worth of a hot technology stock, or logging into my trading account to see that a stock I had taken a chance on was up 50%.

The differences between the typical Saint Mary's students and me hit home very dramatically when, one morning before class, I found myself in the crowded computer lab waiting for a machine to become available. As I looked around, I saw some of my classmates writing term papers or working on school projects, but many others were in chat rooms, emailing friends or playing computer games. I became impatient, angry about waiting, and worried I might not be able to execute the trade I needed to make that morning. I felt my temperature rising as I looked at the occupied terminals and wondered why the other students were wasting so much time goofing around. Of course, none of them knew how important it was for me to access a computer; no one knew I was trading tens of thousands of dollars worth of stock between classes. On the few occasions when I spoke to other students about my trading activities, I realized that I was speaking a language they did not fully understand. If I mentioned the sums of money I was working with, they assumed I was joking, or exaggerating, or even lying. Despite the fact that trading set me apart from most of my fellow students, or perhaps because of it, I kept at it, and I began to make money.

Over the course of twenty months, I did surprisingly well; by 1999, my $25,000 investment had grown to $70,000. There was a slight hiccup in the summer of 1998, during the Asian Financial Crisis and, around the same time, the well-known hedge fund Long Term Capital

Management (LTCM) went bust. This, of course, was the prelude to the 2008 financial crisis, but at the time, I had only a rudimentary understanding of what was going on. It seemed as if smart people were working to solve the problems, and I traded with a sense of confidence. My spirits were high. Then I went home for the summer holidays, found that Euro Disney was trading at 11.20 francs, and I was able to sell my first shares at a profit.

Trading Internet stocks also inspired me to start my own Internet start-up. Some of the people who'd founded the big companies of the day were barely a few years older than me, yet they were worth hundreds of millions of dollars. For example, I remember the IPO of TheGlobe. com, a (money-losing) Internet startup founded by two Cornell students in 1994. The company went public on November 13, 1998. The stock was priced at $9.00 per share and peaked at $97.00 on its first day of trading, creating close to $100 million in wealth for its founders. Those founders were Stephan Paternot and Todd Krizelman and they were both twenty four years old at the time of the IPO.

So in 1998, Ari and I launched 22nd Century Media and Graphics, a design and media company. Ari was not familiar with Web design, but he was artistically talented and once I introduced him to it, his skills quickly surpassed mine. He enjoyed the experience so much, he changed his major from business to computer science.

Even though the company had 'media' and 'graphics' in its name, we really used it as a laboratory to experiment with several website concepts. Our most successful (short-lived) online venture was launched in early 1999; it was a website called Mars Mission, and it sold leases for land on Mars. They were just novelty leases, but our long-term goal was to sell millions so we could finance a mission to Mars and claim those leases for our clients. We sold a handful of leases, the site's traffic was picking up and our excitement was building. Then, a couple of months after the launch, while I was in Paris visiting my parents, Ari took the site off the server to update it. The next day, on April 26, his entire hard disk was erased by the Chernobyl Virus, which was activated in the memory of the Chernobyl nuclear disaster of April 26, 1986. After that, we never really recovered and I turned my attention back to the markets. So I can safely say that I was, inadvertently, a Chernobyl victim—and that I once sold land on Mars.

Back in the markets, things moved smoothly until in October 1999, when I learned a very harsh lesson, thanks to a mistake that was far more damaging than the Euro Disney misstep. It was a trade on a new tech IPO from Efficient Networks, a company that built DSL equipment for high-speed Internet connection. I bought at $90.00, then watched as the stock melted down to $60.00, leaving me with a little more than my original $25,000. One blunder, and every cent of profit was gone.

One aspect of my trading that both amplified my profits and extended my losses was trading on margin. 'Trading on Margin' is when a broker lends you money using your equity as a collateral; the loan could be anywhere from two times to four times the size of your equity. For example, if you had $50,000 in equity, in theory you would be able to take advantage of your 'margin buying power' and invest $100,000 to $250,000. Trading on margin can be extremely profitable for a bullish trader or investor in a rising market, but it is equally devastating when the market turns south.

For me, margin-buying power simply meant free money. I paid no attention to the reverse side of the equation, thus I was fully-margined at all times. Being fully-margined doesn't leave a lot of room to maneuver. When stocks start moving in the wrong direction, a 'margin call' is generated and you are asked to deposit more funds in your brokerage account or sell shares; you usually have three days to comply.

I remember my first margin call—I received a letter from my broker telling me that I had three days to deposit funds or sell stock to reduce my margin exposure. It was a strange letter and I ignored it. Then came more letters, then phone calls. The truth is that I just didn't know what margin calls were. I didn't understand the process, and it took me some time to learn how to best manage them. I had no money to deposit; thus my margin management approach consisted of selling shares to pay down my margin debt or 'praying' the market would rebound. Yet, this never stopped me from utilizing leverage to the maximum extent possible, this is why when I got hit on Efficient Networks my losses were much larger than they would have been if I had only invested cash.

After the loss of my profits, I felt as if everything I had been working for was pointless. I was disgusted with myself; furious that I risked so much without knowing what I was doing, and stunned to find that I had fallen back to earth so suddenly after achieving such impressive gains. I was so utterly repulsed by this failure that I felt I had to change everything about my life, including where I was living. In what is best described as a 'strategic retreat', I decided to withdraw from Saint Mary's, leave Halifax, and go back to Paris to lick my wounds and finish my degree in more familiar surroundings. Before I left Canada, however, I had a chance to make a unique symbolic gesture; one that I hoped would inspire me in the years ahead.

The flight from Halifax to Paris involved a six-hour layover in Toronto. Rather than kill time in the airport, I left the terminal, hailed a cab and asked the driver to take me to 130 King Street West, home of the Toronto Stock Exchange. I had just lost all the profits I had made over nearly two years of trading, but as I walked around Canada's largest financial centre, watching the numbers flow across the giant video screens and soaking in the atmosphere of commerce and money, I felt certain that what I had experienced was only a temporary setback. Indeed, I felt more than confident. I was defiant. I took a deep breath and said, to myself, to the market, and to the world: "I'll be back." It was a moment of overwhelming clarity for me, and I could see that my destiny awaited in the stock market. I was just twenty-one, but I saw my future stretching out in front of me. All I needed was the strength and tenacity to make it come true.

■ ■ ■

Back in Paris, I re-enrolled in Schiller and changed my major from finance to marketing. But the lure of trading was far more compelling than my studies. I still had my initial trading capital, and I again focused my attention on Efficient Networks, even though it had cost me my profits a couple of months earlier. The stock was trading in the $50s and I was convinced that it had fallen too far, too quickly. I knew it was time for it to rebound and I wanted to buy.

I tried to place an online order with my broker, Suretrade. My order was rejected: with the excessive day-trading and the neglected margin calls, they had closed my account and no longer wanted my business. I was unable to capitalize on what I saw as a golden opportunity and it took me a week to transfer to another discount broker, Datek. The delay however, worked in my favour.

The first day I could trade with my Datek account, I found a company called Digital Island. This San Francisco-based web-hosting and content-delivery company processed streaming media for the Web. It was a smaller competitor of Akamai Technologies, a company that had grown large and successful through relationships with Apple and Microsoft. The morning my money first became available to trade with, Digital Island merged with another Internet company called Sandpiper Networks, in a billion-dollar deal that created a company roughly equal in size and value to Akamai. I thought that, as a result of this acquisition, the Digital Island stock was poised to explode in price. Digital Island was trading at $18.00 a share; the stock jumped to $24.00 before official trading started on the merger news.

That same morning I decided to buy the stock, the market was not yet open, and my trading function with Datek was still not activated. So I picked up the phone to make my order the old-fashioned way, placing a pre-market order of 1000 shares at $24.00. I had about $26,000 in capital, so this $24,000 buy-in represented nearly my entire net worth. As soon as the market opened the stock began climbing sharply. In about two hours the shares were trading at $36.00 and I was confident I had made the right decision. My online account with Datek was still not fully functional, and I couldn't check to confirm that my order had executed. I began to worry it hadn't actually gone through. I quickly called my broker, and was informed that, yes, the order had indeed gone in at $24.00. The stock kept rising; by mid-day, it was at $45.00.

By the end of trading, Digital Island settled at $67.00 and I could not resist calling the broker again, just to confirm that I was indeed the owner of a 1000 shares of the stock. It was just unbelievable that I'd recouped everything I'd lost in just one day! My 1000 shares of Digital Island were now worth $67,000, but I chose to hold on to them for a bit longer. This was the right call: the next day the shares hit $80.00, and the day after they were at $110.00. At that point, I sold and wound up with $110,000. In three days, and with a single trade, I had quadrupled my money and regained all of my previous losses.

This was the last week of October 1999. Less than a month earlier, I had stood in the Toronto Stock Exchange and vowed that I would one day re-start my career as a trader. Now, I was stunned by how quickly it had happened. My self-confidence was at an all-time high and the Internet boom was reaching a fever pitch. I began looking for more Digital Island-type opportunities.

During the Tech Bubble of the late '90s, and the first few months of 2000, trading in tech stocks happened in a succession of waves. At first, investors were piling into anything with 'dot com' in the name. A few months later, these same investors had moved on to networking stocks such as Juniper Networks, Extreme Networks and Foundry Networks. A few months after this, they were investing in optical stocks, like JDS Uniphase and E-Tek Dynamics. Traders were jumping from one trending sub-technology sector to the next, moving money to whichever sector was 'heating up'.

Moving money from one type of business to another is nothing new; the market has always been subject to 'sector investing'. Entire industries can rise at once and this rising tide can simultaneously lift the stock prices of companies that are considered to be in competition with each other. For example, if department store stocks are seen as being hot, a rise in the price of Macy's shares will rarely cause a corresponding dip in the price of Nordstrom. It makes no difference that they are in competition; in the market, their fortunes will most likely rise and fall together because they are in the same business.

With stocks like Digital Island and Akamai already trading at rich valuations, I started looking for action elsewhere. One of the sectors that was heating up was optical networking. Canadian optical networker JDS Uniphase was a particular market darling, with hardly a day passing without the stock hitting a new high. Cisco Systems had added further fuel to the fire by acquiring the money-losing two year-old startup Cerent Networks for $6.9 billion (this was a company that had barely made $10 million in sales in the first half of 1999). When a tech behemoth like Cisco pays billions of dollars for a startup, it is a signal that the 'game is on' and money will pour into the sector as investors speculate on who's next. The communication sector was on fire, buoyed by actual or perceived demand for Internet bandwidth. The market capitalizations of companies in the sector grew so large that, at one point, the now-defunct Canadian telecommunication giant Nortel Networks represented around 25% of the entire Toronto Stock Exchange composite.

I figured that optical component maker E-Tek Dynamics was my ticket. It was trading at around $90.00 a share, while its primary competitors like JDS Uniphase and Optical Coating Laboratories were selling for five to ten times as much. The company was profitable and growing like gangbusters. I was sure that E-Tek was poised to ride the optical communication wave upwards, and I bought 1,000 shares at $88.00. The stock didn't skyrocket immediately like Digital Island, but it quickly showed a 10 to 15 point gain. Then it started to bounce around; overall, it was on a steady rising trend, except for the first few days in January 2000, when the market experienced a mini-sell off. But, as always, the market rebounded and took E-Tek with it; by mid-January, the stock was in the $130s and I was sure that a great deal of upside remained.

When I was trading, I hated weekends. There was no action and no money to be made. I was always eager for Monday to arrive, and I typically spent Saturdays and Sundays reading about stocks and chatting with other investors on the message boards. But one week-end was different: on Sunday, January 17, JDS Uniphase announced a stock deal to acquire E-Tek at a 70% premium. As was typical with acquisitions at that time, by market opening on Monday, the stocks of both the company being bought and the company doing the buying were rallying at the same time. My shares were suddenly worth over $320.00, and I promptly sold them.

After E-Tek, I felt I was making serious money. My confidence was sky high, and I had access to close to $1.4 million in liquidity, including my margin buying power. So one day I decided to stop looking for a stock that was moving, and make a stock move myself.

Optical networking stocks were still hot, so I stayed focused on this sector. Given the mania that was then surrounding nearly all optical companies, I knew there was real opportunity and I was certain that if I could find a way to bring some attention to a lagging stock in the sector, it would move. It is important to note that at that time, it didn't matter what a company earned, who managed it or if it even had revenues: it just needed to be in the right sector, or have the appearance of being in the right sector.

Like most traders of that era, I constantly checked the NASDAQ lists, particularly the Gainers List which included twenty equities and ranked the stocks that had made the biggest percentage gains each day. This list showed where the action was so day traders constantly watched it. My idea was to find a stock trading just below the level of the twentieth stock on the Gainers List and, by buying it and upping its price, making it appear on the list. Once it made the list, traders would start buying. It was a simple and elegant idea: nothing speaks more clearly to a trader than the ticker and a rising stock in the right sector.

Scanning the NASDAQ Gainers List, I noticed that the bottom stock on the list was up by about 9%. To get my stock on the list, I needed to move it by 10%. This was no easy feat; moving a stock by 10% requires a lot of capital, and while I had close to $1.5 million to work with, it was a negligible amount in the grand scheme of things.

I had to find a 'micro-cap' stock (micro capitalization stocks are worth under $100 million). It had to be in the optical business and needed to have low trading volume, so that buying it would cause the stock to pop.

I settled on a small, neglected company called Precision Optical. The company made high- precision optical products for the medical industry, but its products also had applications in communication networks and that gave it the appearance of being in the right sector. It had a small market cap and it had the word 'optical' in its name. It was the perfect fit for my experiment.

Precision Optical was trading at about $10.00. To get it on the Gainers List, I would have to move it to $11. It was a risky move: if I went all in and the stock did not move, I'd be stuck, fully margined, in an illiquid stock. But if it worked, and the stock went up, I stood to make a killing.

I started my operation by buying an initial position of 50,000 shares at a bid price of $10.50 (5% above the prevailing price). The stock quickly reacted and traded at $10.5 before sliding back to $10.45. I opted to give it some time to see if other traders would get interested, and some did. Their additional buying quickly took it to $10.70, but it fizzled to $10.55. Worried that these traders would lose interest, I entered my second order of 50,000 shares at $11.00 (again, higher than the prevailing price), and watched as the stock bounced to $11.00, and then weakened to $10.9. That was not enough to get it on the list, but it was close. I decided to use all the money I had left to make a final purchase of 30,000 shares at $11.20. The stock hit $11.20 then fell to $11.10 and stayed there for 20 minutes, just long enough for the stock to enter the NASDAQ Gainers list on Yahoo Finance.

Those 20 minutes felt like an eternity, as I sat wondering if my plan would work, or backfire and leave me stuck with a money-losing optical stock. Then, as if a rocket had been ignited beneath it, the stock shot up. Within hours of entering the list, it was trading at $15.00, then $16.00, then $18.00. It was stunning. For the first time ever, through a combination of capital and my understanding of trader psychology, I had moved a stock up. I truly felt that I earned this gain and I sold my stock that day for a 40% profit.

After Precision Optical, I felt I could not lose. I jumped from one stock to the next at a frenetic pace, making tens of thousands of dollars a day. Though I couldn't find a way to repeat the list maneuver, there were plenty of stocks on the rise, and by March 2000, my net worth was in excess of $640,000. I was the king of the world! I was making money faster and in greater quantities than I could possibly have imagined a few months earlier; it was a surreal experience. Just as in the lyrics from the hit song at the time 'Maria' by Blondie, I felt like "a millionaire walking on imported air".

■ ■ ■

I was proud of myself. I was convinced that I had made this money because I knew what I was doing. At the rate I was making money, I was sure I would be a millionaire within a few months, perhaps even a few weeks. I was fulfilling my destiny, and assured myself that a bright future lay ahead.

Well, within days of hitting my zenith, I would enter into an earthbound descent with no parachute. The Tech Bubble burst. April 2000 saw my wealth beginning to unravel and the onset of some of the harshest days I have ever experienced in the markets. I had to face the bitter truth that my recent success, which I believed it to be the result of my financial prowess and superior investing skills, was simply the product of an unprecedented rise in stock prices.

There is a well-known psychological phenomenon called Confirmation Bias, which occurs when a person seeks out only the information that supports his own beliefs or opinions, and ignores evidence that contradicts them. While the rest of world ran with the story that the market was collapsing and there would be no rebound in the near future, I looked for any news telling me that technology stocks would bounce back and start to rise again. This blocked me from taking my losses and safeguarding the remainder of my capital.

Alas, a rebound was not in the cards, and no amount of hoping, wishing or pretending would erase my catastrophic losses. For the first time, I understood the meaning of a bear market, as stock prices, especially technology stock prices, kept marching down. Day after day, the fall was determined and merciless. On one particularly fearful day, the NASDAQ index fell by over 15% intra-day before recouping most of its losses and closing slightly negative. It was a wild day for my largest position at the time, Extreme Networks. Extreme was an apt name for the ride I went through as the stock rode from the $70s to the $40s, before closing at $69.00. It was one of those days where if you put in a bogus bid at 50% below a stock's price you could well end up owning it.

To add pressure was the fact that some of my friends had invested in the same stocks I was holding—they'd heard of my success, thought I was a 'boy genius' and invested in my picks without question. When the market collapsed and they started losing money, they started complaining. One of my cousins wanted me to buy his shares from him at double their price; many acquaintances severed their contacts with me. Only one, my high school friend Maxim Umnov, did not complain and did not waiver in his friendship, even though he lost several thousand dollars on one of my technology picks. Ten years later, upon the birth of his first child, I sent him a cheque for the amount he'd lost.

As my portfolio shrunk and my losses piled up, I grew more desperate, took more risks, borrowed more margin money and further accelerated my demise. I abandoned any notion of prudence in the hope that I could recover my losses. It didn't work. Every day, the market took back from me the gains I did not deserve in the first place. Between April 2000 and November 2000, when I was finally wiped out, I was like a zombie junkie, fully immersed in my losses. Nothing else mattered. I lost weight, slept badly and withdrew from society—I couldn't face the people who had warned me about the risks of the market, and I couldn't stand those who volunteered advice. After that ordeal, it took me several years to recover and find my footing once again.

5

TORN

Illusion never changed
Into something real
I'm wide awake and I can see
The perfect sky is torn

Natalie Imbruglia

Living in France, I was a Parisian in name only. I loved Paris for its history, culture and beauty, but I never felt connected with the French people. Nor did I feel like a tourist. I was caught between these groups; more than a temporary visitor, less than a native citizen. Paris was like a vast museum: I could walk through it and experience what it had to offer, but I could not be a part of it, and I could never call it home. There seemed to be a pane of glass standing between me and everyone else. I could see them, and they could see me, but there was an invisible barrier between us.

Our apartment was a fifteen-minute walk from the Eiffel Tower. In the summer, the grounds surrounding the landmark were packed with groups of vacationers from around the world, as well as hundreds of vendors, salesmen and con artists hoping to make some easy money off the tourists. In winter, the number of tourists would drop considerably leaving me free to stroll up to the tower, climb the stairs to their highest point on the structure's second level and look out over the city below. Standing there, alone with my thoughts, I could see the very edges of the city as it stretched out and away, with the cold Seine bisecting it. I would breathe in the crisp, chill wind blowing in from the river and relax into a fleeting feeling of serenity and freedom.

The Eiffel Tower was my favourite spot until I discovered the Montparnasse Tower. Opened in 1972, the 59-storey office building stood alone as the only skyscraper in central Paris. Many city residents, who saw Paris as a time capsule preserving an older Europe, hated the tall black obelisk and the progress its construction represented. I thought it was magnificent, if only as a vantage point from which to see the rest of the city. One evening I took a visiting friend to the square observation deck on the building's roof and immediately fell in love with the magnificent vista, a view that is vastly superior to that of the Eiffel Tower. The flat, raised platform in the centre of the building's rooftop offers a uniquely unobstructed 360-degree panorama of the city, including the Eiffel Tower. Perched atop the skyscraper, over 200 metres up, I could lean into the rushing wind and feel as if I was flying above the city, nearly weightless and free as a bird, far removed from the stress and obligations of everyday life.

Back on the ground, in real life, I felt anything but free. I had just gone bust. But while I felt defeated, I remained hopeful that I would eventually come back. In the meantime, I had a lot of hard work to do. I find dwelling on adversity and failure to be uncomfortable and counter-productive—I prefer to shift gears and move forward and, instead of speculating about mistakes or over-analyzing the past, immerse myself in work. I decided I would stay away from investing while I did two things: educate myself about the nature of the stock market and help my father with his hotel business.

I accomplished the first goal by reading classic investing books, seeking out the wisdom and advice of the giants of the investment world. I studied books like *The Intelligent Investor* by Benjamin Graham and *Common Stocks and Uncommon Profits* by Philip A. Fisher. I also read the biographies of famous businessmen like Warren Buffett, George Soros, John D. Rockefeller and J.P. Morgan. What made these men special? How did they think? What did they do to separate themselves from the crowd and become titans?

When I was a kid, I read comic books about super-powered heroes who did amazing things; now I was reading about real people who accomplished things that were no less impressive. They wore suits and ties instead of masks and capes, but these men had used their brains and their will to build empires and fortunes. They profoundly affected the industries in which they worked; they shaped financial systems and, by extension, the world. I knew I had much to learn from their stories and each book I consumed added to my knowledge and advanced my market education.

My second goal was trickier. Father's decade-long foray into the hotel industry had been moderately successful. I gave him enormous credit for his ability to suddenly start over in a new country and a new industry, but I knew the property wasn't coming close to its full potential as a hotel located in one of the world's most popular travel destinations and I was convinced that I could change that. Under my father, the business was limping along; I wanted it to soar. I had completed my BBA in International Business (and won the award for being the best student in the program), so I took what I'd learned about marketing and set to work bringing the family business into the Internet Age.

Like everyone else in 2000, Father was aware that the Web was emerging as a supremely powerful tool for business, but he didn't understand how to capitalize on the opportunity. The hotel did have a rather primitive website, for which he had vastly over-paid. It served as little

more than an online brochure for the hotel and had limited functional-
ity. I decided to design a totally new Internet presence, starting with an
up-dated website that included easy online booking. Then I launched a
campaign to distribute our room inventory through a host of specialized online reservation websites in the vein of Expedia and Travelocity.
I also introduced a number of marketing initiatives, such as paying for
guests' train tickets from the airport to the hotel, and offering free tran-
sit passes for the duration of their stay. We were also one of the first
hotels in Paris to offer free wireless Internet access.

To encourage loyalty and productivity, I introduced an employee
profit-sharing and bonus system, and I allocated auxiliary commissions
from restaurant reservations, cab reservations and show reservations to
the staff. These initiatives worked miracles. Within three years, I had
managed to double the hotel's revenues and triple its profitability. It was
a great validation for me and I believe it elevated my father's image of
me, though he was not a man who was generous with praise.

Of course, this was a French company under the strict oversight of
the notoriously Byzantine and rigid French bureaucratic machine. The
French have a well-known ability to strangle both progress and profit in
vast webs of red tape. Our hotel was regulated by two official agencies,
the Ministry of Tourism and a division within the Ministry of Interior,
and each had its own set of rules, regulations and standards. The codes
of these two separate bureaux were often in conflict: a particular policy
or action required by one agency's rules might put us in violation of
the rules maintained by the other. Since we were officially required to
comply with both, we were constantly walking a tightrope, trying to
please two different sets of bureaucrats whose only real priorities were
to remain in their entrenched and lucrative positions.

The administrative and fiscal burden on the hotel was extremely
heavy. One day, overwhelmed by all of the money flowing out of the
business, I sat down and counted all the taxes, fees and social charges the

French government compelled us to pay. I came up with an incredible fourteen: retirement allocations, health allocations, social allocations, garbage collection tax, music and art tax, professional tax, company income tax, revenue threshold tax, TV tax, advertising and signage tax, value-added tax, training and education tax, property tax and Chamber of Tourism fees. Paying each of these meant dealing with a separate agency, and many required such complex calculations that we had to pay our accountant to prepare and file them. Managing and paying all of these taxes significantly lowered our ability to grow and develop our business. Money, time and effort we should have been spending on attracting new customers and improving the property were wasted in keeping the government machine satisfied.

Another frustration was France's extremely restrictive labour laws. Once an employee is hired full-time, it is virtually impossible to fire him, regardless of issues of insubordination or incompetence. It is more difficult for a business owner to get rid of a bad worker than it is to divorce a bad spouse. This makes the hiring process a bizarre version of 'Till Death Us Do Part', which would be funny if it were not so infuriating. The law does allow for firing employees under certain circumstances but, short of an employee pulling a gun and shooting his boss with twenty witnesses to confirm the event, this rarely happens. France's labour laws are not nearly so restrictive when applied in the other direction, making it fairly easy for a worker to break a contract and leave an employer scrambling for a qualified replacement while wondering if the new employee will be a rotten apple and impossible to fire.

French business regulations can be difficult for native Frenchmen to navigate, but my father was not a Frenchman and had a particularly hard time. Business and government were very different in the Middle East and success for him had nearly always come from playing 'fast and loose' with the rules. In Iraq, he skirted the law and took legal risks, and he continued to do this in France. He often hired workers 'in the black', meaning that he paid them cash and did not declare them to the government. This was extremely dangerous, as we were subject to surprise checks by the police. The discovery of undeclared workers meant a hefty fine, possibly even prison. More potentially devastating, and of particular concern to me, was the possibility that one of these unofficial employees might suffer a serious accident while on the job. Without the protection of a legal employment contract, a workplace injury would leave us open to lawsuits and, possibly, criminal charges. It was a real problem. I recall watching one of our off-the-books cleaning women washing the outsides of the windows of our seven-storey building while standing on a stepladder and leaning out. My heart was in my throat as I imagined her catching her shoe on the window ledge or leaning too far and plummeting to the pavement below.

■ ■ ■

In early 2001, my interest in launching an Internet company was briefly rekindled when I came up with the concept of the Global Travel Exchange or GTX. GTX was built around the idea of trading hotel rooms as futures contracts containing a fixed number of rooms and flexible exercise dates. Tour companies would be able to buy tradable blocks of rooms for an agreed-upon spot price, with delivery occurring on the date at which they booked guests into the rooms. I saw a need in the industry for this product, and even envisaged using it for the airline industry. A college friend, Don Mosley, joined me in the venture, and I enlisted Ari, who was back to his hometown of Manila, to design the website remotely.

GTX got off to a good start. We managed to sign a number of hotel partners and build a basic trading platform, but we were awfully short of funds—with the collapse of the technology bubble, getting startup funding was difficult. Don and I prepared a 100-page business plan and approached every imaginable source for funding, from venture funds, to angel investors to corporations.

Then, on September 11, 2001, Bin Laden brought terrorism to the United States. With the enormity of the human tragedy and the international shock, funding a travel startup became an impossibility. With the near-complete collapse of the travel industry and the fall of technology stocks, nobody wanted anything to do with us. In 2002, we realized that no funding was forthcoming and closed up shop.

In the ensuing years, after the travel industry recovered, I attempted to launch a variety of travel- related websites. Some experienced modest success, but none lived up to their potential. While I was Internet savvy, I lacked the programming skills to build the websites I wanted. I was always dependent on others to bring my ideas to life, and that slowed development and entailed additional costs. Yet the experience gave me valuable knowledge about online marketing, maintaining a visible online presence and being picked up by the search engines—those new marketing skills were of great value in developing the hotel business and my future business initiatives.

■ ■ ■

Working for my father was very stressful. He rarely took my counsel and almost never heeded my warnings; this made for a tense working relationship. In early 2005, against my recommendations, he started to use the hotel as a piggy bank, taking money out of the business and spending it, rather than reinvesting in the business. First, he bought an apartment for my sister, and then he started looking at another hotel property in central France.

I looked at the hotel he was interested in, and realized it was a poor investment. The property was a highway motel with a restaurant attached, in a city called Clermont-Ferrand. The deal excited him as the motel was going out of business and he could snap it up for next to nothing. A friend who ran a nearby restaurant sold him on the idea, talking up the potential profits and offering to manage the motel for us. Father was convinced it was a golden opportunity.

I objected loudly, reminding him that we had absolutely no experience with managing restaurants, or with running highway motels, which are dependent on truck drivers and passing tourists. It was also three hours from Paris by the TGV (high-speed train), which meant that neither of us could be there to supervise. I was convinced that it would be a drain on our resources and I advised my father not to buy it. He did the opposite, emptying our hotel's treasury to make the purchase. It was a bad decision. For the next year, the new property bled money and Father took more and more cash out of the Paris hotel to cover the losses. In just a few short years, the significant profits I had been able to generate for the hotel evaporated and our family business was in a precarious state.

■ ■ ■

With my father negating, then reversing, the upward trajectory I had worked so hard to put the hotel's business on, I turned my attention back to investing. I had been following the market, tracking the winners, losers and overall trends. By early 2003, I had saved $26,000 and decided to dive in again. I was older and wiser and I'd gained plenty of knowledge and insight from the books I'd read. I was confident that I would succeed this time.

My ticket was going to be Charter Communications, a cable provider in which Microsoft co-founder Paul Allen had a large stake. The company had a massive debt, and its stock had been hammered in the 2000 technology rout. With the stock trading at $1.00 from a past high in the double digits, I figured the company was extremely undervalued and went all-in. And having failed to learn my lesson the first time around, I margined some as well. I even convinced Ari to take a position, thereby risking my best friend's money as well. But I was back in the market. I felt alive, motivated and positive that my millions were just a heartbeat away.

Charter traded flat, then dipped to 90c. I started to feel a bit edgy, wondering if the past was about to repeat itself in the form of a huge and sudden loss. But I firmly believed that my analysis was correct. Charter's operations were healthy enough to bring the cable provider's valuation in line with its peers (Comcast or Cablevision), so I stayed put. Sure enough, within a few months, Charter started to turn and, a few weeks after that, the stock had more than quadrupled in value, Ari and I cashed out. I made my stake yet again, and my capital rose to $120,000. I was back where I had been just after my first successful trade in 2000 with Digital Island. It was an enormous and truly satisfying boost to my self-confidence: I still had the golden touch.

From Charter, I went through a series of trades mostly focusing on fallen angels from the tech boom, such as Level 3 Communications and Cisco, and Internet protocol telephone stocks like Vocal-Tech, which were in fashion at the time. By early 2004, my stake had grown to $500,000. Once more, I had run a small stake into a small fortune in a record period of time. I heaved a sigh of relief, as if I had been holding my breath underwater since going bust in November 2000.

Now that I had made my money back, I started thinking about going back to Canada; ever since I started working for my father, I'd had a Canadian immigration application sitting on a shelf above my desk. Canada was my El Dorado, and I was set on going back once I had the means. Little did I know that there would be no Canada, and no lasting relief—not for a long while, as the next two years became the hardest of my life.

■ ■ ■

By early 2005, my market performance was starting to languish. The money was coming too slowly and trading was losing its thrill. Quick success had again lulled me into a sense of invincibility, my investment process became sloppy and I was getting complacent when placing investments. I began to fight against the stagnation by taking bigger risks. After a series of disastrously leveraged investments in companies focused on Internet protocol telephony, my capital had shrunk to $170,000.

Fearing a repeat of the 2000 debacle, I decided to convert my trading account into a cash-only account, with no permissions for options and margins. I twice emailed my broker to request that I be disallowed from buying options and buying on margin, but several weeks went by and the change wasn't made. Having sworn off risky investing, but with my account still allowing me to make these kinds of trades, I was enormously tempted. I felt like a junkie who was trying to quit cold turkey while constantly finding drugs in the house.

I opted to try my hand at options. Options contracts are for risk management, but they are often used as a speculative tool. There are two types of options: a 'call option', which gives the trader the opportunity to buy a stock at a fixed (strike) price at a given date in the future; and a 'put option' that gives the trader the opportunity to sell a stock at a fixed date in the future. Options can be very effective if used properly, but they also can be a risky way to amplify one's buying power without borrowing money. The price paid to buy an option or the income generated from selling an option is called the 'option premium'. In addition to the high volatility associated with trading options, an option has a finite life or what is called the 'expiration date'. When trading an option, you are betting that the underlying stock is going to be at a certain price level on a certain date. Predicting the direction of a stock is hard enough; predicting the direction and the timing is obviously much harder. The expiration date makes options an all-or-nothing proposition: if you make the wrong call, you don't have the luxury of holding on until things improve (as is the case with a stock). A call option that expires above its underlying stock price and a put option that expires below its underlying stock price are worthless.

Having access to options trading, I succumbed to temptation and made a large bet on a company called UTstarcom. UTstarcom was a Chinese telecommunication company that had developed a cheaper cellular phone technology for the Chinese market, similar to a cordless phone with an extended range. The system was invented in Japan and never really took off there but, because of its low cost, it did very well in China. UTstarcom was one of the few technology companies reporting a profit during the technology boom (although this didn't stop the stock from losing 70% of its value when the Tech Bubble burst).

I thought the company was being lumped in with other, money-losing, technology stocks and it didn't deserve the punishment. I initiated a staggered-call options position, which is a series of contracts expiring at fixed dates in the future, at ever-higher prices. Naturally, I was bullish on the company, and if my options expired 'in the money' (with the stock trading at a higher price than the price associated with the option), I stood to make millions. It was a long shot: by the time I got involved, UTstarcom's business was eroding. The stock started to sink and my options contracts expired one after the other, a death by a thousand cuts. By the final cut, my account was reduced to a few thousand dollars. Options had turned out to be just as dangerous and destructive as margin trading and, after this second disaster, it was seven years before I traded options or invested in another technology stock again.

When I lost my final $170,000, I did not dare tell my father. Our relationship was already contentious and I could not face making it worse by admitting my failure. The conflicts we were having about how to manage the hotel were bad enough; I knew he would never again take my business counsel seriously if he thought I had handled my own money incompetently. Later, I would regret this decision but at the time, it seemed like a necessity.

My second fortune-to-bust experience with the stock market was morally devastating. As the saying goes, "Fool me once, shame on you; fool me twice, shame on me". It was abundantly clear that I had only myself to blame for this second failure. There was no tech bubble, there were no exogenous circumstances. I had simply gambled and lost.

When I went bust in 2000, I found refuge in reading and learning about the markets, aware that I was a novice and that I had committed errors that any beginner might commit. This time around, there was no excuse. As I reviewed the litany of mistakes and misjudgments that were of similar nature to those I had committed a few years earlier, it was obvious that I was not as intelligent and talented as I wanted to believe. Yet again, I had disappointed people who believed in me, including my mother who hoped I would become independently successful so I could shield her from my father's erratic behaviour. And my dreams of starting a new life in Canada had evaporated, one expiring options contract at a time.

6

DON'T FEAR THE REAPER

Here, but now they're gone
Seasons don't fear the reaper
Nor do the wind, the sun or the rain

Blue Oyster Cult

By early 2006, the situation was grim. I was working at a job I hated, my stock market fortune was gone, I was in constant conflict with my father and the family hotel business was deteriorating. The second property, which had been a losing proposition from the start, was being managed by a man who knew nothing about running a motel, and Father was unable to check this man's excessive spending. Seeing that my father was struggling, I offered to help, but perhaps due to broken pride, he refused my assistance. Father had kept the second property afloat by sinking an additional 250,000 Euros ($300,000) into it—that was ten times what he had paid for it. On top of that, he had been forced to fire an employee who had taken a full year of sick leave for depression; she sued him for 80,000 Euros as compensation for wrongful dismissal—that was more than double the purchase price of the motel.

Just when it seemed we had hit rock bottom and things could not get worse, they did: my father's health began to crash. At first, his symptoms suggested a simple flu but a two-week course of antibiotics did nothing to help. His ill health persisted through an eight-week business trip through the Middle East, where he was hoping to establish new business ventures. In each nation—Lebanon, Syria, Saudi Arabia, the doctors would make a different diagnosis and prescribe a different treatment. Nothing helped.

Back in Paris, he began to feel even worse. He had always been an energetic man, up early and constantly working. But by the spring of 2006, there were days when he could barely stand. I watched many times as he took a key to an empty room of the hotel and slept there for three or four hours in the middle of the day.

A scan of his lungs turned up a growth, but a biopsy proved it was benign. Still, he got weaker and weaker, and began to look older and older. In July, we put him in the hospital for a full work-up. His doctors performed every test they could think of, trying to find the source of his weakness, fatigue and increasing abdominal pain. Every result came back negative. Grasping at straws for some possible explanation, one doctor even suggested it was stress and that he simply needed a massage.

As Father's health worsened, so did the situation at the Paris hotel. In May 2006, the French government inspected our property for fire safety, ultimately deciding that the building was not up to standard. They immediately stripped the hotel of its two-star rating, an action that instantly affected our ability to attract guests and earn money. Then they said they were setting up a special committee that would, within two or three months, decide if the hotel would be allowed to stay open.

I went to my father with a proposal. We had to convince the government that we were acting in good faith and were committed to making the improvements needed to bring the hotel up to code. I suggested that

I officially take over the management of the hotel, to send a message to the authorities that with new management would come new policies and real change. My father agreed, and I started a long back-and-forth process with the government aimed at keeping the hotel open, reversing its fortunes and staving off disaster.

It was a tricky situation. Without our two-star rating, our revenues were lower. With less revenue, I had less money to make the necessary safety improvements, and therefore less chance of getting the two-star rating reinstated—or of keeping the building open. I had to find some way to break out of this chicken-and-egg cycle. To further complicate matters, the motel property had gone bankrupt and creditors were demanding payment. Hanging in the balance was the Paris apartment where my parents and I lived, and which my father had leveraged to finance the second hotel.

Meanwhile, Father's health was declining. In late July, a desperate visit to the emergency room resulted, once again, in no diagnosis. Then, in August, a friend suggested he try a doctor at another hospital, Hotel-Dieu. On this fellow's advice, we admitted my father, and within a few days, the doctors diagnosed his illness: he had advanced pancreatic cancer, which had already spread to his liver and lungs.

When we got the news, my father's eyes filled with tears. I had seen him tear up only once before, when he and my mother put me on the plane to Halifax, but this was the first time I saw him cry. He had lived through arrest, torture and imprisonment in one of the world's most feared and notorious jails. He had faced the prospect of execution. Yet, to my knowledge, he had never shed a tear. Perhaps because, in the past, however dark the future seemed, there was always some chance of escape, some sliver of hope that he would make it out alive. But on that summer day in Paris, when the doctors explained how far the cancer had spread through his belly and chest, my father knew there was no hope. This time, there would be no escape.

I did not give up so easily. I immediately understood that, in a case this far advanced, a standard course of chemotherapy would be virtually pointless. All it would do was make my father's last months more painful and miserable. Unwilling to abandon hope, I started aggressively searching for any experimental treatments that might offer him a chance of survival.

At the same time, I was running out of time and money to keep the hotel open—this was also vital, as it was the family's only source of income. I did whatever I could to cut operating costs, including cleaning rooms myself and manning the reception desk, all while coming up with a plan to make the required repairs and upgrades to placate the safety inspectors. I was simultaneously working two full-time jobs: manager of the hotel and manager of my father's medical treatments. A full night's sleep became a rarity and time to myself disappeared.

I found a Danish company that was testing a promising experimental treatment for pancreatic cancer, with trials running in Paris. It seemed like the perfect solution but there was a serious problem with the timing. It was August, when Paris empties out as nearly everyone goes on vacation. The doctor running the trials was already out of town; the hospital hosting the trials told me I would have to wait. I knew postponement was not an option—Father was fading fast and needed to start treatment immediately. There was still the option of standard chemotherapy but aside from being of dubious value, it would also disqualify him from the experimental program, which only accepted patients who had not undergone chemotherapy.

I found a second hospital running the trials. Again, the lead doctor was out of town, but the head of oncology was there. He was scheduled to go on holiday; I called and begged him to reschedule his trip, to stay in Paris and put my father through the drug regimen. He refused, saying, "I would love to help you, but I am going on vacation tomorrow". Rather than give up, I resolved to break through. Taking Tamara with me, I went to the hospital, went up to the oncology ward and approached the assistant of the head of the department, asking to speak to the doctor personally. She told me he was due to leave and that the soonest I could see him was in September. I said that by September my father would be dead. Impressed by my persistence, the woman told me to go and knock on the man's door. If he agreed to speak with me, that was fine, but she refused to be involved. This is exactly what I did and he consented to hear me out.

I passionately pleaded with the doctor to let my father have the treatment. He agreed to help. Although he would still be leaving town, he was willing to instruct one of his subordinates in the administration of the drug. Relieved and grateful, I immediately arranged to transfer my father to this new hospital, only to run up into a brick wall. With Father admitted and ready to begin the regimen, the doctor who was tasked with giving him the experimental drug refused to do it. He had concluded that the cancer was too far advanced and that it would be a waste to give my father the treatment. I was stunned and furious, but there was nothing more I could do. With no other recourse, Father began chemotherapy.

Then, another crisis at the hotel. We did not own the property; we leased it from the owners, who suddenly realized that several years had gone by without a jump in the rent. They wrote to say that they were doubling it, and that we could lose the lease if we refused to pay.

The howling wind of my 'perfect storm' of personal and financial problems picked up one more notch. I was simultaneously dealing with a dying father, arrogant doctors, greedy landlords, impatient creditors and stubborn government bureaucrats. It was almost overwhelming, but I had no choice but to tackle each problem in turn, trying to work my way out of this colossal mess one small step at a time.

My first goal was to preserve the hotel's two-star rating, without which the business would be practically worthless. I had to plead my case before a committee of twenty-five people at the *Préfecture*. I had no idea if each of these people had an equal vote or if they reported to someone else who would render a decision, but I stood before them and explained the situation as best I could. I sensed trouble when the head of the committee was unwilling to look me in the eye—while we spoke, he looked around the room as if directing his questions and statements to a non-entity. I had the distinct feeling that, to him, I was not even a person; I was a stack of documents in a file.

While trying to hide my frustration, I told the officials that the problems with the hotel were not intentional, but arose from the fact that my parents, as immigrants who spoke no French, were not fully aware of the regulations. I explained that I had taken over and was working to bring the property up to code as quickly as possible. The committee decided to allow the hotel to stay open, albeit with no star rating, while I made the required improvements. In a few months, they would send inspectors to the hotel and if the committee was satisfied with the inspection report, the hotel would stay open. If not, it would be immediately shut down.

This bought me a little time, for which I was grateful, but it did nothing to solve the fundamental problem: the hotel was not up to code, and I needed to find at least 80,000 Euros to bring it up to standard. That was money I did not have.

This is when my most recent loss in the stock market came back to haunt me. I had never told my father that my 2005 options trading experiment had wiped me out, so he believed I was still solvent. He did not really understand the stock market and was never overly supportive of my efforts to make money as a trader, but he was proud that I was getting ahead. He expected me to finance what was needed to keep the family business open.

I wished I had the money, but I did not and I could not mislead my father on his deathbed. I decided to tell him the truth. It was important to me that he not leave this world believing a lie; he had to know that I had failed as a trader. It was difficult for me to tell him; I felt ashamed, but I found the courage. I also promised him I would save the family business. And his reaction was better than I expected—while he showed a bit of surprise, he expressed his confidence that I would fix everything.

Luckily, for me, in 2006, French banks were flush with cash and lending standards were flexible. I managed to convince my banker to give me a personal loan of 50,000 Euros. I combined this with some of the hotel's working capital and managed to finance the improvements. I did everything I could to bring the old building up to code. In many cases, to demonstrate commitment, I went beyond what was called for: if a hallway needed one fire extinguisher, I installed two; if a floor required three smoke alarms, I put in six. I spent every penny I could scrounge and maxed out the hotel's credit lines to meet the deadline and do everything properly.

There was one major problem: the elevator. Since most buildings in Paris pre-date the invention of the elevator, the lifts were all retrofitted, usually between the stairways. When my father installed the elevator of our hotel in 1992, he was unaware that he needed a special inspection document to certify that the work was done properly. He never got the report and I needed it now, fourteen years later. Without it, we could not pass the overall safety inspection. I approached the proper authorities, who informed me that the report is only issued at the time of an elevator's original installation. They could send inspectors to check the elevator and write a report that would serve the same purpose of certifying the machine's safety, but that report would have a different name and document code. I agreed, and paid 3,000 Euros for the new report. The experts checked the elevator and it passed every test. It was safe.

By October 2006, time was running out, both for my dad and for the hotel. As Father lay clinging to life in hospital, a five-man committee turned up at the hotel for the all-important safety inspection. For hours, I walked these men through every inch of the property, answering questions as they inspected every detail. All the upgrades I had made checked out and as the tour progressed, I began to feel confident that we would pass the inspection and remain in business. Finally, we arrived at the elevator, and I handed over the report and safety certificate. The head of the committee took one look at it and immediately rejected it. The report did not have the correct title, so he would not read it. I explained the report had exactly the same content, and was issued by the same government agency, as the one he was expecting. The only difference was the title. My explanation fell on deaf ears.

A hotel without an elevator is as good as bankrupt. All the safety improvements I made were worthless if they only allowed us to stay open as a seven-storey walk-up. As soon as word got out that guests would have to haul their bags up to their rooms, we would be out of business. Rage boiled inside me as I stood before this uncomprehending, stubborn bureaucrat who had the power to save our family or ruin it with a stroke of a pen. I looked at these bureaucrats, who were squeezing the last ounces of air out of my lungs and refusing to turn the first page of the report and look at its contents, and envisioned throwing them off the hotel's roof.

I suppressed my anger and pleaded strongly with them to open the document. I was determined not to let them leave without having them review the report. Finally, one of the inspectors relented and opened the folder. He quickly saw the inspection I had ordered was even more exhaustive than the one that would have been conducted at the time of installation. The committee chose to accept it.

The hotel had passed and could stay open. I called Father to tell him the news. He could barely speak by this time; his voice was just a hoarse, croaking whisper. But it was obvious that he was comforted knowing that when he was gone, the family would have a business and an income. All of his efforts to build a new life for us in France had been worth it.

Two weeks after the inspection, on October 31, 2006, just before 6:00 a.m., my father died. The chemotherapy was ineffective, as we knew it would be. Only my little sister Tamara was with him when it happened as she wanted to keep vigil that night. My mother took it the hardest, but it was a dark day for all of us.

My relationship with my father had always been complicated; we had more than our fair share of conflicts, disagreements and resentments. In my twenty-eight years, he told me that he loved me only once, and that was in his final days in hospital. I was so stunned I remained silent. I loved him too, despite all his faults and eccentricities, and despite the cool distance that had always stood between us.

Father was gone, but the mistakes he had made while running his business lived on. In early 2007, there were still outstanding loans on the motel property, as well as the short-term loans I had taken out to pay for the safety upgrades. Creditors were circling like hungry sharks. The only money I had was the Paris hotel's 15,000 Euros of working capital, and this was not nearly enough to make the loan payments as well as cover rent and salaries.

Having exhausted all options, and facing the real possibility of filing for bankruptcy, I took an enormous risk. I started day-trading with the hotel's working capital.

■ ■ ■

Everything about that trading decision felt wrong. First, it was extremely reckless, and I knew better. That 15,000 Euros was essential to the operation of the hotel. Losing it would mean the end of the business and bankruptcy for the family.

Another mistake was to go into the market with the goal of making a certain amount of money. It is a truism that the market gives you what it gives you, and it takes what it takes—you cannot begin an investment strategy with the goal of making a specific gain. Mistakes number three and four were my decisions to borrow on margin and buy options, two dangerous strategies I'd never had much luck with. Then there was the larger overall mistake of making investment decisions while under tremendous pressure. If you cannot think clearly and you're panicking, you will not make rational decisions. Desperation leads to unacceptable risks. The more desperate you are, the crazier the risks become.

Almost immediately, my decision to trade with the hotel's money blew up in my face. Within days, I had lost half of it. I was the man of the family, responsible for my mother and younger sister (Tania had married and moved to Sweden). Then I had ten employees to think about. Yet there I was, screwing everything up and digging a deeper hole of debt and loss.

As I sat in front of my computer in my small office in the hotel basement, I had, for the first and only time in my life, something akin to a spiritual experience. I had just wagered all of our remaining money on a far-fetched option trade that would expire in a week. If it went my way, I would make 50,000 Euros. If it didn't, we would be wiped out. And for the first two hours after I made the trade, I sat and watched in misery and fear as the numbers headed in the wrong direction.

All religions have holy figures to which believers pray for specific things. The Mandaean holy figures are akin to Christian saints, and one of these holy men is my mother's great-great grandfather, Saif, which means 'The Sword'. When I was a boy, my mother told me that if I found myself in trouble I should pray to Saif for help and guidance. As an atheist, I would not say that I was praying, but as I sat watching my last hope dwindle away on the computer monitor, I found myself talking to Saif. I asked him for help, and told him I didn't know what else to do. I also made a promise: this would be my final trade. I wasn't doing this for myself... it was to save the family, the hotel and its employees.

Call it coincidence or divine intervention, but just as I finished talking to Saif, the market made a sudden and dramatic turn. For my short-term options to pay out, the stock I was betting against had to collapse. The faster it collapsed, the faster my profit would rise. As I watched with widening eyes, I saw the stock I was betting against go into freefall, earning me money with each downward plunge. By the end of the day, I had made 46,000 Euros, or about $75,000. This was just enough money to cover the hotel's short-term debts and keep the business functioning while I worked on a long-term plan—a sane plan.

Still, the business was still drowning in red ink and I had to perform a delicate juggling act with creditors. A few of the lenders let me reschedule payments; but others were more rigid and wanted their money right away. In one case, I was forced to bluff and tell a creditor I was in the process of moving the family back to Iraq, where I could ignore the debt—if he didn't accept a percentage of the total amount owed, he'd get nothing. He accepted.

Erasing another debt required even fancier maneuvers. My father shared a large loan with a business partner; they had borrowed money from a beer distributer. As soon as my father died, this man transferred all his assets to his wife and told me he was broke. This was unacceptable. I would take responsibility for my father's share of the debt, but I would not let this man use a dirty trick to steal from me. I could play just as rough.

My first move was to write a letter to the beer company, offering to reschedule only my father's share of the debt. They responded with a letter refusing this offer and demanding the full amount owed. I replied with a plan to pay off the full amount through monthly installments, and the company wrote back, agreeing to this proposal.

Then I met with my father's former business partner. I showed him *first* letter to the beer distributor, in which I offered to repay only my father's share of the loan. Then I showed him the beer company's response to my *second* letter, in which it accepted my installment proposal. By coincidence, the correspondence was worded in such a way that pairing the first proposal with the second response made it look like the beer company was willing to divide responsibility for the debt, accept repayment of my father's debt and hold his partner responsible for the balance. The man grudgingly agreed to pay his share. I am not fond of subterfuge, but he had tried to cheat me and deserved being on the losing end of what, for me, was a creative solution to a problem.

I was eventually able to pay back 80% of the hotel's total debt and obtain write-downs on the rest. The Clermont-Ferrand motel was taken over by creditors, but it was money-losing property anyway and I wasn't bothered. In 2008, under my management, the Paris hotel had a record-breaking year of occupancy, revenues and profits. It had been a long, hard struggle, but everything was finally in order. The business was in the black, and future prospects looked stable.

By 2009, feeling that I had done my duty to the family and not wanting to spend the rest of my life as a hotel manager, I sold my share of the business to my mother for half its value and chose a professional director to assume the responsibility of running the business. The family's affairs were in order, and they would continue to earn an income from the hotel property without having to deal with the day-to-day decisions.

It was time for me to start the next chapter of my life. I was free to move to Canada with a clean slate. My new life was about to begin.

7

SWEET DREAMS

Sweet dreams are made of this
Who am I to disagree?

Eurythmics

On Christmas day 2008, nearly ten years since my solemn oath at the Toronto Stock Exchange, I arrived in Vancouver. I was ecstatic to be back. I have loved Canada since my days in Halifax; the country is vast and beautiful and its people are friendly and welcoming. Canadians didn't ask where I was from—they didn't care. France never felt like home—Canada did; it was a place where I could build my life.

My fresh start in Canada was also to be a new start in the stock market. Despite two stints of success and failure, I still felt destined to make it big in the market. This time, I was going to play it right. I was going to avoid excessive margin borrowing, avoid option trading, avoid tech stocks and focus exclusively on old-world industries such as real estate and oil and gas.

I also had capital vastly larger than I had ever access to before: $800,000, which was the combined total of my share of the hotel and the proceeds from the sale of my house in Baghdad. This house was the only asset the Saddam regime hadn't taken from my family; the land had been registered under my name when I was five, and the house was built on it after my father was released from prison. During the Saddam years, it was impossible to sell property and move the money abroad, so the house remained empty, then occupied by my father's relatives (who rented their own house while living in mine for free). After Saddam fell in 2003, real estate prices skyrocketed in Baghdad. My first instinct was to sell, but my father's family refused to leave. Finally, in 2005, they moved out—and handed the keys to squatters. I got rid of the squatters by hiring an army unit, something that was, incredibly, possible at the time. Yet, it took three years, and thousands of dollars in taxes, bribes and commissions to empty that house.

The real estate deal was definitely unusual. I placed an online ad that was seen by the assistant to an advisor to the Iraqi president. Then, after a few weeks of negotiation, the advisor came to Paris on business and we met at the *Hôtel de Crillon* by the Place de la Concorde. He handed me an envelope full of cash as a down payment and we shook hands on the deal. A few months later, I received the reminder of the funds, but not before I had to transfer the title of the house. It was a tense forty-eight hours between the title transfer and the receipt of my funds, as I was handing the buyer the keys before I got the full payment. I had no choice but to accept those terms; he was the sole interested buyer.

People thought I was practically giving away the Baghdad property, but the price of the house was irrelevant—what mattered was the price in relation to other assets, such as stocks and commodities. Those other assets were trading at extremely low valuations due to the fear and chaos caused by the financial crisis. I wanted to deploy the house proceeds in the stock market, which was in freefall as the 2008 financial crisis unfolded. I sensed this crisis was a unique and historic opportunity to invest.

I was undeterred by the fear felt by most investors at that time. I had been through enough to know this state of affairs would not continue:

the world economy would recover, confidence would return, fear would give way to greed and stock prices would rebound. I was investing cash, so there would be no margin calls to squeeze me out. I would not invest in options and risk having them expire with no value. I would stay away from technology stocks, and the possibility of watching as their technological discoveries became obsolete. I was going to invest in boring but vital industries. I had learned my lessons from the past, through an education that had cost a million dollars in 'tuition'. By December 2008, I knew that education would pay off big-time.

One of the sectors I focused on in my third foray into the stock market was oil and gas. I grew up in a country that was highly dependent on oil and I believed this gave me a special awareness of this strategic commodity. When I was a kid living in Baghdad, my father and I would often talk about oil production and oil prices and he would tell me what he knew about the industry. As a director in the Ministry of Industry, and as a businessman, he had always been interested in oil and minerals. He taught me the difference between light oil and heavy oil, between Brent Crude oil and West Texas Intermediate oil, and explained the reasons for varied extraction costs in the oil basins of the world. I remember these discussions as eye-opening and thought-provoking lessons, but also as rare pleasant times spent with my father. Some fathers and sons talk about baseball or cars; my dad and I bonded over business.

In 2007, I became Peak Oil-aware. The thesis of oil production reaching its maximum rate made tremendous sense to me, and it was obvious that the world was running out of cheap oil. Several countries had peaked in very quick succession—the U.S. in 1970, Indonesia in 1977, the U.K. in 1999, Norway in 2001 and Mexico in 2004. The world was steadily transitioning to more expensive oil such as Alberta's Oil Sands, Brazil's deep-water reserves and tight/shale oil in the Unites States. To me, the future was clear: as total conventional oil reserves shrank, the emerging world oil demand would steadily grow. Oil would come from more labour-intensive sources, oil prices would steadily rise and well-managed oil companies would continue to offer great opportunities for investment.

Critics of the Peak Oil theory point to OPEC's vast stated oil reserves, but I have always been suspicious of those calculations, which I believe owe more to politics than science. I am particularly skeptical of the 322 billion barrels in reserves added between 1982 and 1988 (cited by BP data in Morgan Downey's *Oil 101*) once OPEC had partially tied production quotas to the size of its member-country reserves.

My knowledge and interest in oil was a key factor in helping me decipher the noise from the facts during the financial crisis, and when oil prices dipped to $39.00 dollars a barrel in late 2008, I invested heavily in the sector. My research showed that the marginal cost of a barrel of oil was at least twice the price of oil; the cost of a barrel of crude at the Norwegian North Sea was as high as $75.00, shale oil required a price of at least $60.00 a barrel (today it is closer to $90.00), and an even higher price was needed for the Canadian oil sands. OPEC countries required much higher oil prices to fund their ever-rising domestic budgets, which further signaled that a price near $40.00 was far too low and surely temporary.

Despite all of this, the financial media was cluttered with doom-and-gloom predictions of a continued decline in oil prices, and investment houses such as Merrill Lynch were calling for a price as low as $25.00. That did not make sense—it was evident that prices were self-correcting and that supply would shortly shrink until prices were high enough to allow for the marginal supply to hit the market. The only security I looked for was investing in companies whose balance sheets were solid enough to withstand the pressure until prices reverted to the marginal cost. I was confident of a rebound but it was impossible to know exactly when that rebound would happen.

The company with which I chose to gain exposure to the oil industry was a small Chinese operation called China North Petroleum, one of the new companies created after the limited privatization of the Chinese resource industry in the late 2000s. As was the case with many of its peers, China North was trading at a very low valuation—its oil reserves were valued at under $2.00 a barrel. It was also a low-cost oil producer benefiting from cheap Chinese labour and easily-accessible conventional reserves. It had no debt, and it was in the process of being listed on the NYSE Amex. The company was trading at around $2.00 a share, yet my analysis of its cash flow, assets and growth prospects indicated that the stock should have been trading in the double digits. It looked viable, I was bullish on oil prices, and I was bullish on China, so I invested heavily and with conviction by putting half my assets into the company.

As the stock market headed towards its March 2009 bottom, the stock languished. But by May, as oil prices rallied towards $80.00 a barrel, the stock started to show signs of life then raced forward, hitting $10.00 in January 2010, when I sold out. This was a massive win for me, and it confirmed that my new strategy of investing in undervalued companies without utilizing margin or gambling with naked options could still yield substantial returns—in this case, in excess of 500%. I felt a strong sense of pride and accomplishment as I transformed $400,000 into $2 million.

This satisfaction was diluted over the next two years though, when it turned out that China North Petroleum was nothing more than a fraud: its numbers were found to be fabricated, its executives were indicted and its stock was delisted. While I had invested in this company for the right reasons, and shown prudence, foresight and patience in my approach, I had never thought of the risk of fraud. I had this naïve belief that, after the Enron and WorldCom scandals, public companies were better scrutinized, and that NYSE Amex-listed companies underwent in-depth vetting.

China North was certainly not the only fraudulent Chinese company; scores were uncovered between 2010 and 2012, and many investors lost fortunes. I was simply lucky, but I was equally annoyed that I had publicly discussed the stock on my blog in 2009 and 2010. Some anonymous Internet posters even accused me of colluding with China North's executives, a baseless but harmful accusation. The China North episode added the risk of fraud to my long list of possible dangers; I have not invested in a China-based company since.

■ ■ ■

Investing in a stock, or a basket of stocks, entails making a certain number of assumptions about how those investments will perform in the future. Of course, the reality may differ from expectations; a stock that is supposed to increase in price may stay flat or decline before eventually moving in the right direction. Time can become the enemy, so it is unwise to invest capital that may be needed in the near future, or to utilize excessive amounts of leverage that may force an untimely position liquidation. As John Maynard Keynes said, "Markets can remain irrational a lot longer than you and I can remain solvent." When it came to placing new investments in 2008 and 2009, I was careful to have the resources to withstand an extended period of negative performance.

Investors who utilize heavy margin borrowing also limit their ability to withstand adverse price movements. They may actually be forced to sell at the worst possible time as their brokerage houses demand their money; in most cases, margin agreements allow a broker to simply go into the trading account and liquidate assets. This is why I stayed away from margin trading in my third foray into the stock market; even though I eventually introduced some debt, I never deployed it to the extent of my early years.

■ ■ ■

People often compare the markets to war; powerful forces and participants fight each other to gain wealth, power and control. In the 1980s, books like Sun Tzu's *The Art of War* were all the rage, and investors and traders employed all weapons and tactics at their disposal to prevail. Usually, victory was measured in terms of dollars but, in certain instances, it was more about power, reputation and control.

Growing up in Baghdad, surrounded by war, I loved to play at war, building elaborate installations and properly positioning my soldiers, tanks and planes. Twenty years later, I was still playing with plastic soldiers but now the battlefield was the marketplace. I saw the dollars in my portfolio as my soldiers and, with each investment or trade I would commit some of my forces to battle. If I was victorious, I would capture enemy soldiers (more dollars) and draft them to my cause; if I lost, my men would be sacrificed. As with all generals, I wanted more soldiers, more resources and control of more territory. If a battle turned sour, I would opt for a tactical retreat, or bring in more troops to hold the threatened front.

I'm not saying that investing or trading is a game—it's not, but we need passion and imagination to pursue our goals. I could not engage in an activity if it was devoid of the need for creativity. Investing, especially value investing, could be one of the most boring professional pursuits: buying an undervalued and inactive stock and waiting for it to appreciate is like watching paint dry. Taking a colourful approach towards investing allowed me to maintain a certain level of excitement in the exercise of my profession.

■ ■ ■

By the time I arrived in Vancouver, I understood that investing was not a game of numbers. Numbers are obviously important when analyzing a balance sheet or reading an income statement, but to be a successful investor, I also had to master the emotional side of my brain.

Any investor with a slight understanding of the numbers would see the sense in buying marquee stocks like Dow Chemical, Google or Amgen at a fraction of their value during the financial crisis, but how many investors did buy? More importantly, of those who bought, how many held on? Some did, but I'm sure that many others did not. The reason people don't make money in such circumstances is not because they are unable to understand numbers, but because they don't understand themselves. They don't understand that fear is a more powerful emotion than greed and that the herd mentality comes more naturally to us.

One of the sectors I focused on during the financial crisis was real estate, specifically Real Estate Investment Trusts (REITs). I had invested half of my capital in oil and gas; I invested the other $400,000 in REITs. I figured that, no matter how bad the economy got in North America, it made sense to replace real estate in Baghdad with commercial or industrial real estate in Canada. I eventually also rolled the money I gained from my oil investment into this sector.

I looked for REITs that were trading at a sharp discount to their net asset value, with reasonable leverage ratios and sustainable dividends. Some of the REITs I identified, such as H&R and Dundee, were trading at 30% of their net asset value. While there was some risk that funding might dry up for these trusts, the upside was still substantial because the value of their underlying assets widely exceeded their market value, even if we applied a significant discount to the underlying value of their real estate holdings and assumed a fire-sale liquidation.

Investing in REITs turned out to be the best investment move of my career, mainly because I had the foresight to sit and wait for those companies to rebound to their true value after the panic subsided. My gains were 20%, 50%, even 100%, yet I continued to hold on and refused the temptation to book in a profit. I knew that investors would be searching for yield and would be worried about inflation due to the massive easing and money-printing undertaken by the world's central banks. I waited patiently and enjoyed the dividends. Eventually, I sold those REITs for gains ranging from 100% to 400%, reaping millions. A study conducted in Taiwan between 1992 and 2006, and published in 2010 by the University of California under the title *Do Day Traders Rationally Learn About Their Ability?*, found that short-term traders are twice as likely to sell their winning stocks as they are to sell their losers. My experience has taught me that reversing this bias is an effective way to significantly enhance investment returns.

I should explain my approach to the actual buying or selling of stock. While I always have a valuation target in mind, I don't dwell on selling or buying at an exact price—I focus on a price range. For example, when I acquired H&R REIT, it was trading at $4.80 per share. I didn't care if I paid $4.80, $4.85 or $4.79; the stock was already too cheap to worry about spending a few pennies more. As long as the price is within a reasonable range from my target price I buy it, and the same goes for selling. I can't count the number of times I have had investors tell me about missing great runs because they refused to pay an extra penny.

The REITs episode drove home one of the key lessons of my investment career: let profits run. It is vital to resist the urge to trade out of a winning position, as long as the foundation for that trade or investment remains valid and the investment is progressing as expected.

In 1923, Edwin Lefèvre published a novel called *Reminiscences of a Stock Operator*. It was a thinly disguised biography of the famous American securities trader Jesse Livermore who says,

"It never was my thinking that made the big money for me. It always was my sitting. Got that? My sitting tight! It is no trick at all to be right on the market. You always find lots of early bulls in bull markets and early bears in bear markets. I've known many men who were right at exactly the right time, and began buying or selling stocks when prices were at the very level that should show the greatest profit. And their experience invariably matched mine—that is, they made no real money out of it. Men who can both be right and sit tight are uncommon."

This stands true today for the simple reason that the human brain has not evolved. We continue to be the same as people who traded in 1923, and we will be the same a hundred years from now. We may have high-speed computers, but our software remains the same and we respond to fear and stimuli in the same way as did our ancestors tens of thousands of years ago.

Patience is another key to obtaining superior returns in the markets. If patience was a commodity, it would be trading at an all-time low. It is frowned upon, with most investors looking to make a lot of money quickly—according to Alan Newman at Crosscurrents, the average holding period shrunk from four years in the period 1926-1999, to three months between 1999 and today. What many investors fail to understand is that real business operates at real-life speed. Managers still need to analyze, execute, research, motivate and plan; employees still need to crunch numbers, build widgets and serve clients. Staff must deal with regulations, with the limitations of the physical world, and with a day that is only twenty-four hours long. Major accomplishments take time to happen. Investors must remember that no great company was created overnight, and no great fortune will be built overnight.

One reason patience is so difficult to practice is that investors are constantly bombarded with 'news'. Business news networks have one job: to spit it out. If it's unworthy, they make it sound worthy.

In truth, most of the daily flow is useless. Business news networks create the impression that the business world is full of excitement, with mergers and acquisitions, ever-changing economic statistics, analysts upgrading and downgrading stocks and star managers shuffling their holdings. It is all of little value. The fundamentals of any company or industry take time to develop, and the really valuable information doesn't come from a media 'scoop'; it comes from methodical research. From talking to a company's executives and its competitors, reading industry publications and regulatory filings, and debating the merits of the company with people you trust. Real-time news media may have a role for day-traders or swing-traders, but investors who watch business channels need to resist the temptation to act or extrapolate from short-term phenomena. Differentiating between noise and real business information requires perspective and training; experienced investors develop the ability to tune out the noise.

One of the biggest generators of noise is the army of analysts. Analyst reports can be useful in providing factual information about a given business, but they are generally useless in terms of projections and price targets. The fact that an analyst knows how to plug numbers into spread sheets does not mean that he is an oracle—it just demonstrates that he knows how to use Excel. Analysts are no better qualified to predict the future of a company than an investor who is willing to do the meticulous research work while putting his or her money on the line. Furthermore, Analysts are often disadvantaged since they are usually restricted by working relationships and the pressure to conform with 'the street'.

■ ■ ■

Then there is randomness, an aspect of life that fascinates me. What would my life had been if we had not left Baghdad when we did? What if Saddam Hussein had never invaded Kuwait and we had been able to return from Europe?

In my stock market trading career I have been both blessed and cursed, I have had amazing success and crippling failures, there is no doubt that luck and randomness had their part to play. The fact that the Internet was born as I was coming of age offered me the chance to embark on this journey; obviously, it gave me the technology boom, the tools to trade and the right environment at the right time.

Back in the spring of 2001, as I was still recovering from my first major loss in the stock market, and even though I was helping my father at the hotel, going to school and tinkering with online ventures, I took the time to get involved in online chats. One day, I came across the screen name 'Evelien' and initiated a conversation. I learned that Evelien was a girl of about the same age, living in the Netherlands. We chatted for a few weeks, and then she said that she would be visiting a friend in Paris and I gave her my number. She called me twice and left messages, but she had no cell phone so I couldn't call her back. The following day, three hours before her train would take her back to Amsterdam, she tried a third time and reached me. We arranged to meet at a bench near the Arc de Triomphe. And there I met the most beautiful girl I have ever seen. She was tall with aqua eyes, long blond wavy hair and she had an amazing graceful air. I was immediately smitten. Three days later, I took the train to Amsterdam, where we had our first kiss. We have been together ever since and I can't imagine what my life would have been without her—I shudder to think what life would have been like if I'd missed her third call.

Those who believe in a creator think that what happens in their lives is the will of that creator. I see life in terms of randomness, and as the ongoing outcome of decisions made by me, and countless others that have nothing to do with me.

Some argue that the same random theory applies to the stock market. Share prices move as a result of the decisions of countless of participants; those participants are divergent in their views, in the speed at which they make decisions, and in the scope in which they can make decisions. This is consistent with the random walk hypothesis, which argues that stock prices change randomly and cannot be predicted. The concept dates back to 1863, when it appeared in the book *Calcul des Chances et Philosophie de la Bourse*, by French economist Jules Regnault. In 1900, the theory was further developed by the French mathematician, Louis Bachelier, who used it in his PhD thesis *Théorie de la Speculation*. In the 1960s and 1970s, it underwent further discussion, by MIT Professor Paul Cootner and Burton Malkiel at Princeton.

Eugene Fama, the Nobel laureate and University of Chicago professor, also agreed with the random walk concept in his PhD thesis *The Behaviour of Stock Market Prices*, which was published in the January 1965 issue of the *Journal of Business*. Fama added to the subject when he postulated the Efficient Market Hypothesis (EMH), which he first discussed in his article *Efficient Capital Markets: A Review of Theory and Empirical Work*, published in the same journal in May 1970. EMH argues that asset prices are always reflective of all available public information, thus investors are unable to out-perform the market over an extended period. Psychologists Daniel Kahneman and Amos Tversky, and behavioural economists Richard Thaler and Robert Shiller, have argued strongly against the EMH thesis, and value investors such as Warren Buffett have repeatedly demonstrated the ability of value investors to outperform the market over decades, thus discrediting the EMH thesis.

While I have not done empirical research, my observations as a market participant make me an ally of the EMH dissenters. I do not believe that all investors reach the same conclusion to a given piece of information at the same time. Not all investors are in a position to act on a given piece of information, and not all information is disseminated at the same speed to all investors (especially in small-cap illiquid securities.)

Throughout my investment career, I have witnessed investors both in a state of fear and euphoria. I have seen the many factors that can influence or impair the judgment of market participants, such as experiencing a winning streak, experiencing a large loss or coming across a large amount of money. I know that my emotional state has affected my investment decisions on more than one occasion, and my investor acquaintances have said the same. My own experiences and observations are highly indicative of market inefficiency.

Yet, not withstanding skepticism of the efficient market hypothesis or the randomness of the markets, it is undeniable that value investors are inherently believers that markets are ultimately efficient. Without such a belief, companies with distorted stock prices may never reach their true valuation. I reconcile the two through what I call the 'Cyclical Efficient Market Hypothesis' (CEMH), or "the point where the intrinsic value of a security converges temporarily with that security's market price".

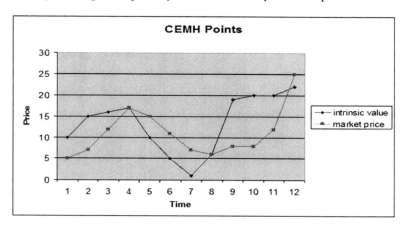

When I invest, I aim to buy stocks at the point of maximum negative divergence between the stock price and the company's intrinsic value, and sell when both values converge. Thus, while I define myself as a value investor and accept that the value of a given stock often diverges from its real value, I am a firm believer that, over time, a company's true value would be reflected in the stock price (albeit temporarily).

Temporary fluctuations in stock prices may very well be random, or they could be due to instantaneous efficiency as each new piece of information is processed. But it can't be ruled out that such fluctuations may also be due to investor inefficiency in the processing of information, investor inefficiency in acting on this information or investor inefficiency due to an aroused emotional state. I recognize that accepting the randomness of life and yet rejecting permanent randomness in the movement of stock prices may seem to be an oxymoronic position. Yet, I believe my position could be reconciled by my belief that while major and small events may change the course of a human life and a society, human nature never changes. Humans are both able logical thinkers and flawed emotional creatures, and stock prices reflect that.

In 1637, at the peak of the Tulip mania in Holland, people bought almost worthless tulip bulbs for the price of a mansion. In 1999, investors bid up the price of Internet stocks, issued by companies that had made no money and were unlikely to make money, to valuations often exceeding those of the blue chips. In 2013, a digital code of unknown origin masquerading as a currency labeled Bitcoin was bid to over $1200 a coin (and may very well jump several folds higher before imploding). Trading vehicles change name, shape and colour, but the price action never changes, and will never change because it is driven by human nature. While everything around us is pretty much random, human nature is not. Even though I am fascinated with the randomness of life, my investment returns are predicated on the predictability of human nature or as I like to call it "emotional arbitrage".

All of these lessons and insights drove my eventual success as I dove into the market for the third time. I was patient, I let my profits run, and I focused on the proper valuations and business fundamentals. I didn't buy stocks per se, I bought "companies". I had been humbled by the markets in the past and was now open to advice and criticism. I shied away from margin trading. I strove to be objective and I worked with passion and determination.

I had to get it right because I knew this was my last chance. In the past, I had had a cushion to fall back on—my father's business, my Baghdad property. Now there was nothing. Plus, failing would mean wasting the best investment opportunity in my lifetime. I was now successful beyond the wildest dreams of many. By 2011, my initial stake of $800,000 had been transformed into a fortune in excess of $8 million. I was at the top of the world—wealthy, living in one of the most beautiful cities in the world, engaged to the love of my life and in the company of great friends in my adopted country of Canada. I had finally touched the stars I had spent so many nights silently observing from our humble roof in Baghdad.

I was also aware that despite all of the great lessons I had learned and applied since 2008, I had been helped tremendously by a roaring market. I was smart enough and brave enough to pull the trigger in the midst of financial crisis. But would I survive the next crisis? Would I manage to out-perform in a stagnating market? Would my old demons of excessive risk and hubris rear their ugly heads once more? In the next couple of years, I found out that climbing to the top was the easy part. Staying on top was the real challenge.

8

STARLIGHT

Far away
This ship is taking me far away

Muse

I believe that my choice to live in North America was no accident. Many of the people who discovered this land were pioneers—people who were seeking adventure and a better life, and had the courage and conviction to pursue their dreams. Unfortunately, in the public at large such people are the exception and not the norm. It is such a shame to see people constructing artificial walls around their heads—walls that artificially hold them within imaginary boundaries setting out what they could and could not achieve. Those who build these imaginary prisons have a harder time escaping them the longer they confine themselves. Some say the easiest person to fool is yourself; I believe the easiest person to imprison is yourself.

Humans are born with a capacity to imagine and wonder. With time, though, this thirst to wonder and explore gives way to comforting ritual. The famous French high-wire artist Philippe Petit, who made eight crossings between Manhattan's Twin Towers, said, "I cannot kill the child in me. I refuse." I have found this to be true of most great innovators, leaders and entrepreneurs; those who refuse to kill their inner child end up dazzling the adults.

This is why, when I achieved my financial goals, I was afraid that I would lose my drive to go further. I was worried that I would be imprisoned by my wealth—that it would own me. For a short while, it did.

My wealth gave me security, and it gave me the freedom to pursue life as I wished without being beholden to anyone. But this freedom was only an illusion because you can't be free if you are fearful. Being oblivious to this basic fact, I made the decision to stay away from the market and all its risks, and seek an alternate business career—not just to avoid risk, but also because I found the prospect of continuing to make money for the sake of accumulating it void of substance. My new career had to offer two things: lower risk, and meaning.

I began by looking at the arts. As noted, my mother was a gifted artist, but I did not inherit her talent for drawing and painting. She did, however, instill in me an appreciation for art and the creative process, and I had a long-held interest in making movies; in high school, I briefly wanted to become a film director. So I commenced investigating the world of independent filmmaking, hoping to find a project that was both potentially entertaining and culturally significant. Vancouver is one of the busiest film production centres in the world, with television shows and movies constantly shooting on its streets and in its studios. It was not difficult to find people interested in making a film, especially when I made it known that I had substantial funds to invest.

My mental picture of filmmaking was a bit idealistic. I was very much interested in the creative side, but as I delved deeper into the industry, I noticed it was more about business than art. Navigating through the process of funding a movie, I started to feel like a cow being milked, with the nagging suspicion that the people around me were more charlatans than artists. The shiny lure of the glamorous world of movie-making worked for a few weeks, until I understood that this was a business where it is nearly impossible to separate the gold from the tinsel. As I explored and debated the various projects coming at me, I realized that I had no clear understanding of the movie industry and couldn't trust my own decisions. The exercise quickly became more of a burden than an activity in which I could find meaning. I decided to keep the magic in movies and TV shows by watching them on screens. My career as a film producer was over.

Next, I looked at becoming a venture capitalist. I could use my wealth and my business experience to support interesting startups. I had long admired those who become angel investors. I had dabbled with my own online startups and I understood the frustrations of trying to launch a project without the proper support and funding. This could be a noble and satisfying calling, I thought. I figured I'd look for potential in underfunded businesses and help build them into something stronger and better. I might discover the next diamond-in-the-rough and use my capital and experience to help polish it into a jewel!

I spent several months shopping for prospective candidates. I considered companies in social gaming and got very close to funding a company that could have been the next social gaming colossus. I backed out when I discovered that this company only wanted to raise funds to screw a shareholder by buying back his shares on the cheap before signing a major deal with a new distributor. Then I considered a number of companies in the alternative energy sector, but quickly saw that their survival was due more to government subsides than to the merits of their business plans.

Choosing a startup was made more difficult by the fact that my stock market investment philosophy was focused on old-world businesses with stable cash flows. I was increasingly risk-averse and no company could impress me enough to override this elevated caution.

Plus, I had the feeling I might very well end up throwing money at people who had no interest in working hard or building anything unique or meaningful. I ended my search and put the idea of venture capitalism on the cold back burner.

I began to worry that I might strike out. What if I could not find a road that led to happiness and fulfillment? I needed to reassess my situation. What were my core skills? What was I truly good at? I certainly had a great deal of experience in the hotel business. I had transformed my family's Paris hotel from a barely-functioning mess into a steady income-producing success. The effort had combined all my different interests and abilities, from creative marketing and PR, to financial planning, to staff management. Perhaps I could replicate this success in Vancouver, which is both a business capital and a tourist destination.

There were dozens of large hotels, and lots of available real estate offering the prospect of building more. But the more I thought about this idea, the gloomier I became. I was once again falling into the trap of equating success with fulfillment. Yes, I had been a successful hotel manager, but I had done that for my family. I had been miserable. The hotel was a burden and I had spent a lot of my time dreaming of escape. I could not go back to that. I would not risk spending a decade, or even a few years, in a career that would very likely end up making me angry and frustrated. If monetary success was going to be the only upside, it would be no better than where I currently was as an investor.

In early 2012, I was back to square one and tiring of this career search. The truth of the matter was that trading the markets, learning about them and investing in them is what I had been doing since I was a teenager, and the passion of being part of the markets could not be replaced.

This is when I started to toy with the idea of activist investing. It felt like a natural next step—why shy away from the markets when I finally had enough wealth to make my voice heard? It was my passion for investing and risk-taking that had brought me this far; perhaps this same passion and drive would take me further still. I just had to get better at the game and use what it has to offer for a better purpose. The answer to my search was in the markets, not outside of them.

Activist investors use their stakes in companies to enact change in the way those companies do business. In the 1980s, such investors were often called 'corporate raiders' and were seen in a negative light. The management of the companies they targeted, aided by a hostile press, painted them as greedy bullies who gobbled up and broke apart healthy companies in their mad lust for profit and glory. Investors like Carl Icahn and T-Boone Pickens were vilified as unfeeling pirates or soulless capitalists out to make quick billions with no concern for the consequences of their actions.

Around the turn of the 21st century, many people began to understand that such investors could play an important role in the operations of publicly-held companies. They can provide a much-needed check against entrenched management teams who become blind to the rights of their investors and deaf to investors' pleas for change. Shareholder activism, when done for the right reasons, is not only beneficial, but also essential to the health of the financial markets and the economy as a whole.

After my first bust in 2000 and my subsequent thrust to further my understanding of investing, I read a great deal about activists, but they were a world apart from where I was. To be an activist, you needed millions of dollars and, to be effective, you had to have a reputation or track record. By 2012, I had half of that—I had enough money to be effective in a small cap setting, but I didn't have a name and my activism philosophy was still immature. The big question was what kind of activist I wanted to be. Did I want to be the 'bad guy', inserting myself in a company's business for personal gain and fame? Or did I want to act for the right reasons, as a 'constructive activist'?

Constructive activist investors remind executives, boards and the public that publicly-traded companies are accountable to their owners. When a company flounders or strays from its mission, activist investors make sure that the company is put back on the right path and that the business is managed in a fashion that will maximize returns for the true owners of the company—the shareholders, as opposed to their agents, their executives and their board members.

CEOs and directors of public companies are supposed to make business decisions to serve the interests of the people who pay their salaries, their shareholders. If hundreds or thousands of investors had to vote on every decision made by a company in the course of doing business, chaos would reign and nothing would ever be accomplished. So investors elect board members, who hire and oversee executives who have the skills to lead and manage the affairs of the company. The directors bear a heavy obligation to shareholders to act in shareholders' best interests. At least, this is how the system is meant to work.

I realized years before I thought about activism that this is not how the system actually works. History books are filled with stories of politicians who were elected by promising to serve the needs of their constituents, but they were actually serving their own interests of consolidating power, making fortunes, and staying in their positions as long as they could. Politicians often say whatever they need to say to get the job, and then, once in office, ignore their promises and pursue strategies of self-interest. This phenomenon is even more common in the business world. Increasingly, the executives running many publicly-held companies have abandoned the notion of serving the needs of shareholders, and have adopted strategies that primarily serve to preserve and protect their own power and income.

Chief Executive Officers, particularly those of large companies, have always been well paid for their labour, and few would argue that they don't deserve above-average salaries and benefits for their high-pressure positions. It makes sense that the captain who steers the ship is paid more than the man who shovels coal below decks, as the captain's job is not only harder to fill, but requires more training and specialized knowledge. The captain is also the public face of the ship, and therefore held to a higher standard than most workers.

But there is, or should be, a limit. According to the Economic Policy Institute (EPI), in the 1960s to mid-1970s, a typical American CEO was paid about twenty-six times as much as the average production worker. Nothing to sneeze at, and those salaries guaranteed these men lives that were more than comfortable. They held big stressful jobs and they were rewarded with big salaries and bonuses. If executive compensation had remained at this level, I would have little to argue with. But it didn't stay at that level. As Forbes reported in 2011, by the century's end, CEO pay had shot up and people in the same jobs were earning 200 to 300 times as much as the average worker. According to the EPI, from 1978 to 2011, average American CEO compensation increased by 725% against a 349% rise in the S&P Index, a rise that boggles the mind and clearly has little to do with job performance. In 2010, *USA Today* reported that the top 500 US executives pulled in a combined total of $4.5 billion in compensation, averaging $9 million each. The Institute for Policy Studies found that twenty-six of those executives earned more money than their respective companies paid in federal tax!

Canada has experienced similar trends. The Canadian Centre for Policy Alternatives found that, between 1995 and 2010, the compensation of the top fifty Canadian CEOs jumped from 85 times the average worker's pay, to 255 times that amount. As a matter of fact, between New Year's Eve 2013 and 1:00 p.m. on January 2, 2014, the top 100 Canadian CEOs had each earned about $46,634.00—or what the average Canadian worker earns in one year.

Human nature is prone to greed. This is a simple fact, and it's why modern societies have developed sophisticated systems of oversight in political and economic institutions. Left unchecked, people tend to act out of self-interest. It's a behaviour that has been rewarded for thousands of years and temptation remains hard to resist. But the level of avarice and selfishness exhibited by contemporary executives, and the complacency of their enablers, have reached worrisome levels.

The extraordinary thing about the CEO/C-suite compensation levels is that boards of directors approve them all. At a certain point, the level of compensation is positively detrimental to the success of the company and the interests of shareholders. That means that, by approving these extraordinary compensation packages, the directors could be in breach of their fiduciary duty.

The cozy relationship between senior corporate executives and their boards is not well understood. In my many years of trading and investing, I have researched hundreds of corporations. I have pondered the nature of business trends big and small, and I have spent countless hours crunching numbers, and reading financial statements to gain insight into both individual companies and entire industries. Yet, it has only been in the last two or three years that I have asked myself a simple question: how do directors get their jobs? How do these men and women (mostly men) gain access to the immensely powerful bodies that control our public companies?

I have repeatedly asked other investors if they know how the board members controlling their investments actually got their positions. The answer is almost always the same: they don't know. In most cases, only the board members themselves know how they got their jobs. As far as I can tell, nobody goes through the labour-intensive process of figuring out how individual board members come by their seats. Even experienced activist investors who pick apart companies to determine precisely what is and isn't working, rarely know how and why board members are selected. These people just appear at the top of corporations, and investors almost never question it.

There is the argument that board member selection is unique to each corporation, therefore board development cannot be discussed so broadly. In certain instances, board members are chosen based on their reputations or expertise in a specific field. Sometimes the choice stems from social or professional relationships with the CEO or Chairman; sometimes a board position is a reward for a service rendered or is part of a strategy involving a possible future merger or transaction.

The core issue is not just about who is chosen, but who does the choosing. The current system is structured so that, in the normal course of business, only the existing board's nominating committee is able to nominate a candidate to the board. If this were a political system, the system would have only the exiting government filter/choose the candidates to run against it in the next round of elections, which would make a mockery of the democratic process.

It wasn't always like this. There was a time not too long ago, when companies were founded by people with true vision who built on their ideas, nourished the private business institutions they brought to life, and eventually took them public to raise money and remained engaged with them—people like Henry Ford, Bill Hewlett and Dave Packard, Bill Gates or Google's Larry Page and Sergey Brin. Those founders ran their companies with purpose and determination, and as large shareholders they shared in the ups and downs with their fellow shareholders. While founders still run some companies, many public companies have lost touch with their founders and, at the board level, have been transformed into retirement clubs for senior businessmen. For many, board positions are a means of staying connected, keeping power and influence, or simply have something to do besides spending the severance packages they took when they left their last jobs.

Often, directors lack any real ownership in the companies they serve, holding a token stake of a few hundred shares. In practical terms, this lack of financial commitment translates to a lack of incentive. They are like retail salesmen who have neither ownership of the store nor commission on sales: there is no reason for them to do their best, because neither success nor failure affects them. Of course, there are some board members who attempt to do good for the sake of preserving their reputations, and who take their fiduciary responsibilities seriously, but in my experience, these people are the exception rather than the rule.

During the 2008 financial crisis, it became abundantly clear that the board members of many American companies, especially banks and financial institutions, were asleep at the switch. The directors were unable or unwilling to make decisions on their own. For the most part, they merely gobbled up whatever advice the bank executives gave them. In the end, many of the world's most respected (or formerly respected) institutions went hat in hand to the U.S. government to bail them out, while the boards, supposedly made up of the best and brightest businessmen in the capitalist world, shrugged their shoulders and acted as if there was nothing they could have done differently.

The board members' indifference, often amounting to negligence, is not entirely their fault. Passive and apathetic investors are disconnected from the underlying businesses of the companies they own. If they don't hold directors accountable, those directors will often support management. I blame part of this apathy on the current short-term focus exhibited by many investors. Institutions and hedge funds are trading algorithmically, holding stock for mere moments. Retail investors are put into stocks by brokers who don't conduct thorough due diligence. The pension funds and mutual funds habitually vote for board nominees by giving their proxies to management; this is partially due to the structure and the misaligned incentives within the financial industry.

Retail and institutional investors of previous generations typically viewed buying stock as buying pieces of the businesses that issued that stock, so they took an interest in how those businesses were managed. There was a perception of ownership going beyond the daily ups and downs of the tickers. Investors understood that, over the long term, good business practices produced consistent profits and strong dividends. Investors held their shares for years and tied their own fortunes to how these businesses prospered, or failed to prosper, in the real world. Now, with the average investor holding shares for an average of just three months, stocks are just pieces of paper and numbers on a screen; profit and loss is seen as a function of trading these pieces of paper from week to week and day to day, and little or no attention is paid to how companies operate. Increasingly, investors see themselves as traders rather than owners. Their portfolios change and shift so often and so quickly there is no time to understand the companies they own, let alone form opinions about policy or initiate contact with management. With the focus on the ticker, transaction decisions are based on equations rather than business strategy. Investors are here today and gone tomorrow, never showing their faces, and never sticking around long enough to care what goes on behind the scenes. This quick turnover creates the impression of an ownerless enterprise, which in turn motivates boards to ignore investors altogether.

The consequence of apathetic shareholders and complacent boards of directors is that many companies grow decadent. Issues go unresolved. Piles of debt are accumulated, piles of cash are hoarded, unproductive assets lie moldering on the balance sheets, and executive compensation becomes too sensitive for discussion. 'Sound management' becomes a rationale for maintaining the *status quo*. Nothing changes, issues are left for another day and, bit by bit, shareholder value melts away.

Good directors, and there are many, are often as frustrated as the shareholders they represent. Gwyn Morgan, former CEO of energy giant Encana, resigned as board chairman at SNC-Lavalin after the company became embroiled in bribery scandals. As he told *Boulevard Magazine*, the scandals "emphasized the difference between being CEO and being a board member. When you're CEO, you know what's going on and everything is at your disposal. When you're on a board, every bit of information you get comes from the company, so you have this fundamental limitation."

This has elements of truth, however nothing stops a director from asking hard questions. Nor is there anything to stop a director from actively listening to the shareholders of the company. Directors are there to safeguard shareholder interests; finding out what those interests are is part of the job. Sadly, relatively few investors make sure that directors are aware of their responsibilities.

It took about a year for my ideas on activism to fully form. The more I pondered the matter, the more activism emerged as a perfect fit for me—constructive activism, that is. It was an activity that had meaning, and it had a true utility beyond the simple fact of making money by passively investing in companies or speculating with their stock. Yet the fact that activism entailed getting involved with the companies I would target also meant that I could reduce my risk by playing an active role in shaping the outcome of my investments.

9

SMELLS LIKE TEEN SPIRIT

I'm worse at what I do best
And for this gift I feel blessed

Nirvana

As mentioned, the period between late 2008 and the middle of 2011 was exceptional in terms of investment performance; I had gathered a multi-million dollar fortune and, between dividends and capital gains, my annual income was in the millions. But as 2011 progressed, my performance started to flatten and I lost interest in passive investing. My interest in activism was not fully developed yet. One cold December day, I decided to try something I had never done: buy a million shares in a sizeable public entity and single-handedly underwrite its valuation for one day. That company was Gasfrac Energy Services.

Gasfrac is a hydraulic fracturing technology and service company. Hydraulic fracturing, or 'fracking', is the process of injecting millions of gallons of chemically-enhanced water and sand into an oil or gas well in order to break the rock and release the hydrocarbons. Gasfrac was involved in the same process, but instead of using water as a carrying fluid, it used propane.

I found the technology fascinating. The process appeared to be more effective than water fracturing, much less polluting due to the limited use of harmful chemicals, and more sustainable because of the conservation of water. Gasfrac used hydrocarbons to unlock hydrocarbons; I believed that this process would ultimately dominate as it was adopted in North America and around the world, yielding Gasfrac tremendous profits and a much higher stock price.

My interest in Gasfrac's fracturing technology was only half the story; some of the old demons of complacency, impatience and vanity were the other half. The spark that awakened those old demons was Europe.

In late 2011, the European sovereign debt crisis was starting to come to the forefront and market volatility came with it. I was sitting on the sidelines, but I had the constant feeling that I was missing out. Having made a fortune capitalizing on the financial crisis three years earlier, I felt I should capitalize on this one too. Eager to join the action, I started to buy small positions in more speculative stocks that were getting hit as a result of the increase in volatility.

I identified Gasfrac as one of those stocks. The company was trading as high as $14.00 less than a year before, and there it was at $6.50. After doing some research on the technology and the company's financials, I felt comfortable enough to buy a small position of 80,000 shares.

Meanwhile, my income portfolio, which was heavily weighted to oil stocks, started to crater. This further added to my discontent and the guarded approach to investing which I had carefully nurtured over the past three years started to give way to speculative hunger. I felt that I was still young and ready to hit it big, or bigger than I had so far. Those long-buried speculative urges that got me into investing in the late '90s returned to convert my brain cells to their cause.

At 2:00 a.m. on December 14, 2011, my younger sister Tamara called. She was on her way to visit me and was at the airport in Paris. I had put her ticket on my credit card, and the airline wouldn't allow her to board because the ticket was purchased with someone else's card. The airline told me I had to go to Vancouver airport to show my credit card to one of their agents. By 2:45, I was at the airport; to my surprise, no one was there, because no one starts until 4:00 a.m. I was extremely angry, but after a series of calls to the airline and my credit card company, I managed to get my sister on her plane. I got back home at around 4:30 and slept until 6:30, getting up in time for the market's opening (something I have done since I began as a day-trader).

That morning, Gasfrac stock, which had been doing little but bouncing around since I bought it, opened down more than 4% and was trading in the low $6s. The combination of minimal sleep and several months of frustration with my portfolio and business career led to my decision to do whatever it took to support Gasfrac's stock price. In hindsight, it was an insane and irrational decision, but I was overwhelmed by the temptation to *be* the market, rather than just be *in* the market. I even went to the Gasfrac's message board on Yahoo Finance, where I usually chatted with fellow shareholders, and declared that I was going to single-handedly support the stock and close it in positive territory. I said, "I'm going to close this stock in the green."

I kept my word. By the end of trading, I had liquidated many of my other investments and acquired one million shares of Gasfrac for $6.7 million, adding 920,000 to my existing 80,000. My buying was 90% of Gasfrac's volume that day and the stock closed 1.3% higher against a negative tape. I had prevailed against the market; the torturing beast was tamed. But just for that day—it would eventually come back to exact vengeance.

Over time, I convinced myself that Gasfrac was going to be a major success. I started to believe this was a real investment and not just a speculation. In January 2012, I published a detailed article about the company on the financial news and blogging website Seeking Alpha.

The article was read over 20,000 times and caused the stock to rally sharply. I was not just a passive investor; over time, I published a dozen detailed articles about the company as I conducted my own research and uncovered further facts about the company.

Finally, Gasfrac's share price started to move in the right direction and, in late February, it touched $9.00. I was up over $2 million in just two months. I sensed that I should lighten up on the stock, but I also felt that this would betray my investing principle of letting profits run (even though I had betrayed every other principle since I made the Gasfrac trade). Worse, I felt I would be betraying all those investors and friends who bought the stock on my recommendation. Something was telling me I needed to exit the stock, but I chose to ignore the feeling and stay in.

Soon after climbing to $9.00, the stock started to fall back. Concerned that the company's business was not performing well, on March 15, I called the company's CEO, Zeke Zeringue.

Zeringue, an industry veteran and one-time president of Halliburton's Energy Services Group, was pleasant enough to speak with. He knew I was a big supporter of the company and expressed appreciation for my work. But I felt he was not being straight with me. When he talked about the company and its future, there was more 'hope' than facts. To be fair, he did speak about the challenges of introducing a new technology, and the issues surrounding the aftermath of a recent fire at one of the firm's wells. But he had nothing enlightening to say and didn't offer anything that wasn't already available to the investing public.

When I hung up the phone, I felt there was something wrong and I knew I needed to immediately and completely exit my position. I had a powerful urge to sell at any price. Once again, though, I suppressed my instinct and bought into the CEO's positive message about the future of Gasfrac.

Four days later, the company warned of sub-par quarterly results and the stock sunk by 12%. Less than a month later, the company warned again; the stock sunk by another 22%. Suddenly, I had a $3.7 million loss. By the end of April, the stock risked dropping below $5.00, when it would automatically become a penny stock, which many institutional investors are prohibited from buying. I opted to exit the stock and use the funds to advance an activist campaign at another company.

Exiting Gasfrac at $5.00 was the right decision; it saved my fortune, as the stock eventually collapsed to under $2.00. Despite the loss, I was actually proud of myself for having had the courage to take that loss. One of the hardest decisions an investor can make is the one to take a large loss—most investors don't want to sell a losing stock and will hold on in the hope that it will rebound. If I learned anything in the years of investing prior to getting involved with Gasfrac, it was that it is critical to cut one's losses once the facts show that a company's situation has changed. I had let hope stand in the way of action in 2000, and again in 2005, and I was proud of myself for not repeating my mistake.

Looking back at the Gasfrac episode, I realize that the biggest danger to my portfolio was me. By 2011, I believed that my investing demons were gone, and they were not. I made big mistakes. I gambled on an unproven technology, bought a big chunk of a company out of vanity, refused to heed the advice of many who warned me about the viability of the company, put too much faith in a management body that had not proven itself in a small enterprise, and remained invested in the company for reasons other than those directly related to the validity of the investment.

The Gasfrac Debacle, as I call it, put the final nail in the coffin of my interest in any technology investment. Moreover, it ingrained in me the priority of minimizing the risk of loss by looking at the possible downside of a given investment first and foremost, rather than at

124 THE BULL OF HEAVEN

its potential upside. Or, as Warren Buffett says: "Rule No.1, never lose money, Rule No.2: never forget Rule No.1".

With the Gasfrac Debacle behind me, I was ready to jump with full force into the most sophisticated and complex financial battle I have ever fought—an activist campaign against a TSX/NYSE-listed Canadian energy company. It was the first battle I undertook based on my newly developed activist ideology and it would define the next two years of my professional life and test every ounce of my intelligence, patience, determination and courage.

10

SPACE ODDITY

Ground Control to Major Tom
Your circuit's dead, there's something wrong
Can you hear me, Major Tom?

David Bowie

In 2011, Calgary-based Equal Energy was an unremarkable energy company which produced 10,000 barrels a day of hydrocarbons: 50% natural gas and 50% liquids (ethane, propane, butane, pentane and crude oil). It had a relatively small market capitalization of $200 million, with assets in Canada and the United States, and it was listed on both the Toronto and New York stock exchanges. Equal's CEO was Don Klapko, who had been appointed to the post in June 2008 after working as a consultant for the company since late 2007. To my knowledge, Klapko had no prior executive-level experience in running public companies.

When I first came across Equal, I saw a company trading at a very low valuation, which was less than half that of its peers and less than half its own net asset value. While the company had a relatively high debt level, I felt the stock was oversold. I knew that natural gas prices had collapsed due to surging shale gas production in the U.S.; and that, combined with a warmer than average winter that year, was going to have an effect on a natural gas-weighted company. However, Equal's peers were experiencing the same difficulties, yet they were not punished by the market to the same degree, and their stock did not trade at the same vast discount to net asset value. Equal's management maintained that the decline in the stock price was purely the result of low natural gas prices; my analysis indicated deeper problems.

Initially, my investment in Equal was conducted along the lines of traditional value investing; it evolved into a full activist endeavour played into by the factors I discussed earlier, and factors that were unique to Equal.

Value investing is predicated on the belief that certain businesses trade at less than their intrinsic or actual value. Value investors reject the idea that the stock market is, as economists put it, 'efficient', with 'efficient' meaning that all of a company's information is captured, more or less perfectly, in the price of that company's shares. Value investors believe that the stock market can misprice stocks, or entire sectors, and for a wide variety of reasons.

For example, the 2011-2012 European financial crisis punished North American stocks, particularly the Canadian oil and gas sector. Companies within this sector had been sold off across the board; to a value investor, the sector was 'oversold'. And a broad sell-off of an otherwise healthy sector may present significant buying opportunities.

Once a sector has been identified as having been oversold, value investors start to look at companies within that sector, and look at their relative or intrinsic value. If the overall sector has declined by 20%, companies whose value has declined by 40% or 50% could offer significantly better returns when the sector returns to a normalized valuation. However, for a value investor to do well, he has to ensure that those declines are caused by the volatility in the market rather than problems with the company; if companies are valued cheaply because they should be, they are called 'value traps'.

A company is subject to a multitude of challenges. Some of those are beyond management's control: a sudden spike in interest rates, a decline in the prices of its products, innovations that make its products obsolete. In this case, a reduction in the price of its shares will reflect an actual decline in the value of the business. However, some issues are within the company's control: the wrong asset mix, the failure to invest in the future, taking on excessive debt or erroneous capital allocation. In this case, a decline in the value of the company's shares reflects the shortcomings of management and their inability to address ongoing challenges.

A company doesn't necessarily have to have an actual problem (either beyond or within its control) for its shares to sell off, but only a perceived one: this could be due to the market underestimating the potential for its product(s), undervaluing a sub-segment of its assets, or overestimating its financial, legal or environmental obligations. Companies that are under-valued because of perceived problems are the most attractive for value investors. Some companies are mispriced for external reasons, such as a major shareholder's needing to sell shares. Indeed, the mere presence of a major shareholder with financial difficulties can be enough to depress share value, and this sort of situation is a boon for the value investor.

For a traditional value investor, a company with a depressed valuation due to controllable causes offers an opportunity. Assuming the company has qualified management, a value investor can take a hands-off approach and wait for management to address the underlying causes for the undervaluation; once the problems are fixed, the stock price should rise to it proper valuation.

Activist investors make the same valuation calculations as value investors, but they often lack the same confidence in management's ability to address challenges, especially if management is the company's biggest problem. As noted activist investor Andrew Shapiro, founder and portfolio manager of San Francisco's Lawndale Capital told me, "All activists are inherently value investors, but not all value investors are activists."

If you owned a business that was losing money or market share, you would not sit back and let your employees try to figure things out; you would identify your company's problems and actively intervene to fix them. It is your business and, as the owner, you have a direct stake in its success or failure. An activist investor follows that same logic.

There are obvious differences of scale between a small business and a public company with millions in market capitalization, but the principle is the same: an owner can and must take an active interest in the management of the business he owns. Regardless of the size of the company, it is critical that the owner knows his business, and identifies problems and their potential solutions.

The principles of value investing and the possibilities of activism in the energy sector are no different than the principles governing those issues with other businesses, except that the energy sector has a few unique specificities.

To be viable, energy companies need to continuously replenish their oil or natural gas reserves, because their reserves are their main asset. 'Reserves' are the (finite) amount of product in the ground, and they must be replenished through the drilling of new wells. When you own shares in an energy company, you own a proportionate share of those reserves, and have a claim on profits as reserves are proven, developed and produced. Reserves are classified in three categories:

Proven Producing: These are wells that have been drilled and are producing. They are usually the most valuable for an energy company, as they're proven and require only slight maintenance capital to keep them producing until they run dry.

Proven Non-Producing: These reserves have been identified, but not drilled. They usually offset producing wells, and have adjacent facilities such as pipelines and processing plants that can transport and process their eventual production. This category of reserves is the second most valuable for an energy company.

Probable: This category is the least valuable, because these reserves have a 50% chance of being there, and extensive capital for drilling and production infrastructure needs to be invested to prove and produce them.

An energy company also has to maintain production, with production levels determined by how many wells are operating, and at what capacity. The nature of oil and gas production means that as an energy company produces its hydrocarbons, that production steadily declines as the reserves are drained and the pressure in the oil and gas formation diminishes (there are ways to slow production declines through secondary recovery techniques such as water-flooding and CO_2 injection). The decline rate can vary according to technical factors, and can vary from the low single digits to over 50% per year. Thus, to maintain its reserves, an energy company needs to keep drilling wells to bring in new production and offset the decline in production and reserves. A growing energy company needs to go beyond reserve and production replacement by drilling wells at a faster rate than the rate of its reserve depletion.

Of course, beyond production and reserves, any business is about generating cash flow, and energy companies are no different. The cash flow of an energy company is a simple function of how much cash it is generating from the sale of its oil and natural gas, and how much it is spending to drill new wells and maintain old ones, plus overhead—salaries, professional fees, office costs and the expenses involved in running a public company.

This appears straightforward, but the energy business is complicated by the fact that the price of oil and gas is volatile, and a manager needs to effectively manage costs and adjust drilling and development plans in an ever-changing pricing environment. One way that energy companies deal with changing energy prices is through hedging their production, which is selling a portion of their production at a fixed price at a future date to guarantee a certain amount of cash flow and thus reduce the risk of a significant dip in revenues if energy prices weaken.

Regardless of the business of a company, its purpose is to generate a profit for its owners—a sustainable profit. A company that generates profits at the expense of reinvesting in its facilities is not making a sustainable profit. Without long-term re-investment, the business will deteriorate. It will fail to remain competitive; it will erode in value and will ultimately generate a loss for its owners.

Measuring the performance of management in an energy company is really about gauging how well it manages reserves and cash flow. A useful way of doing this is to measure performance on a 'per-share basis'. A share in an energy company gives its owner a claim over the company's assets, so what a shareholder cares about is that reserves and production are rising on this basis. A shareholder's stake can be diminished by an action of the company; this is called 'dilution' and it is one of the biggest threats to a shareholder.

Say that you live in a household of two and collectively earn $100,000 a year. Your mortgage is fully paid and your house is worth $500,000, your car is worth $20,000, you have no debt and you have $30,000 in savings. What is your household's net worth? $550,000. What is the net worth of each house member? $275,000. What is the income of each household member? $50,000.

Five years later, your household has grown to five people with total earnings of $120,000, your house is worth $600,000, your car is worth $10,000, you still have no debt and you have $50,000 in the bank. The household net worth has increased by 20%, and household income has increased by 20%. But when we look at the wealth and

income of individual household members, we see a decrease of 52%—
the net worth of each person is $132,000 and their share of income is
$24,000.

To put this in public company terms: if, in its first year, a company
has assets of $10 million, income of $1 million, and 10 million shares
outstanding, the value of each share is $1.00 and the per-share income is
$.10. Say that management issues 15 million shares to acquire an asset.
If that asset is worth $15 million and produces $1.5 million in annual
income then, on a per-share basis, nothing changes. However, if the
asset acquired is only worth $5 million and only produces $500,000 a
year in income, the asset value of each share will be $.60 and the per-
share income drops to $.06. The total assets and the income of the com-
pany will increase, but the shareholders will be worse off.

If it wants to, the management of an energy company can mislead
its investors by constantly focusing on the absolute growth in reserves
or production of the company, without discussing growth or production on a per-share basis. It can keep issuing shares to the public in
order to acquire more reserves and increase production, but if that
increase does not keep up with the number of shares issued, existing
investors are actually getting poorer, and the stock price will keep
declining while the company maintains the appearance of improving
operations. This means that it's crucial for investors in energy companies to demand that management communicate performance on a
per-share basis.

On June 30, 2010, Equal Energy had 21.97 million shares outstanding. By June 30, 2011, it had 34.66 million shares outstanding, an
increase of 11.69 million shares. This increase in share count did not
bring with it a commensurate increase in reserves, production or assets.
So even though management claimed that the company reserves and
production were growing on an absolute basis, the holdings of Equal's
shareholders had been diluted.

Equal's management was adept at playing this game of obfuscation. Under the leadership of Don Klapko, there was a significant quantifiable destruction of per-share value in all key metrics: shareholder equity, production and reserves which saw declines of between 16% and 56%.

This is illustrated in the following graphs, which cover the period of my observation, up to the end of 2012, and use information derived from the company's public filings.

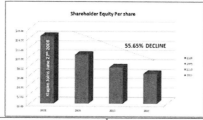

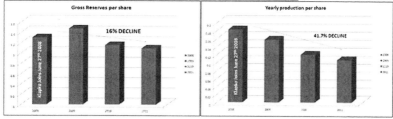

What you see here was not apparent to lay investors as, year after year, Don Klapko maintained the appearance of adding value to their shares, as demonstrated in assertions made in his annual and quarterly shareholder letters. In his 2010 shareholder letter, for example, Klapko claimed that Equal had "increased (our) reserves booking year over year," yet closer examination showed that per-share gross reserves *declined* from 1.47 barrels per share in 2009, to 1.15 barrels per share in 2010. In his 2011 shareholder letter, Klapko stated, "In 2011, production volumes averaged 10,142 boe/d (barrels of oil equivalent per day), an increase of 11% over 2010," yet I found that yearly per-share production *declined* by 16.7%: from 0.12 barrels per share in 2010, to 0.10 barrels per share in 2011.

It should be noted that there is nothing fraudulent about the CEO's statements; they are perfectly true and legal, but they are misleading because they only tell a portion of the whole story.

Equal's financial and production results, as the facts showed, were dismal. They indicated a high level of incompetence or neglect on the part of management in relation to the creation and preservation of shareholder wealth. It is possible that Equal's management team members genuinely believed they were doing their best, and that these operational shortcomings were not of their own making. Also, if given a choice, all managers will try to communicate results in the best light.

Further, we can't expect management to police themselves; that is the job of the board of directors. That is what troubled me: why had Equal's board not acted to protect shareholders? A simple way to keep management on its game is to align executive compensation with performance. The board of directors sets executive compensation; for years, Equal's board permitted demonstrated underperformance and obfuscation of the facts, while awarding the CEO millions in compensation.

Right from the start, Klapko was very well paid. As a consultant, Klapko was paid $840,000 for his seven months consulting services; when he became CEO in June 2008, he received a $4 million cash-signing bonus. In its 2009 circular, the board justified this by saying that he served the company well and was much sought-after and thus such a high bonus was appropriate.

According to calculations taken from information circulars issued by Equal between 2008 to 2012, Don Klapko's total compensation during that time was $10.54 million. During the same period, shareholders experienced a 55.65% decline in per-share equity, a 16% decline in per-share reserves, and a 41.7% decline in per-share production. In 2008 alone, Klapko's total compensation was over $6.5 million, including $2.3 million in share-based compensation. According to *Alberta Venture Magazine,* his pay for that year (excluding share-based compensation) was more than what was received by the CEOs of Canadian Oil Sands Trust and Canadian Natural Resources, two companies that are up to 300 times larger than Equal Energy.

For 2011, the year after which I commenced my activism, Klapko's compensation was 424% higher than the previous year, while the company's top executives saw pay increases of 45% to 84%. This despite a 30% drop in the share price, a 21% decline in per-share equity, a 13% decline in per-share production and a 5% loss of pre-share gross reserves for that year. The longer shareholders ignored it, the more blatant became the gap between results and compensation.

In the 2011 information circular, in an apparent effort to justify this compensation, the board issued a list of largely meaningless goals as accomplishments by the CEO for that year:

List of Equal Energy CEO Goals & Accomplishments for 2011
(Copied directly from the company's circular)

1. Led and managed the Corporation and its subsidiaries within the parameters set by the Board of Directors and its committees.

2. Developed and recommended the corporate strategy.

3. Directed and monitored the activities of the Corporation and its subsidiaries in a manner that focused on achieving the strategic, operational and capital plans of the Corporation and on safeguarding and optimizing the assets of the Corporation in the best interests of the shareholders.

4. Reported to the Board of Directors regularly on actual results compared to planned objectives.

5. Developed and implemented operational policies to guide the Corporation and its subsidiaries within the framework of the strategic directions adopted by the Board of Directors.

6. In conjunction with the Chief Financial Officer, designed and oversaw the effectiveness and the integrity of the internal controls and management systems of the Corporation and its subsidiaries.

7. Identified, to the extent possible, all significant risks to the Corporation's businesses and considered and established, where appropriate, procedures to mitigate the impact of the risks in the best interest of the shareholders of the Corporation.

8. Managed the marketing function, while operating within the Board-sanctioned risk profile and Board of Directors approved financial instruments, with the objective of optimizing the overall returns for the Corporation.

9. Ensured that the Chairman and other directors had access to management necessary to permit the Board of Directors to fulfill its statutory and other fiduciary obligations.

10. Fostered a corporate culture that promotes ethical practices.

11. Established a process of supervision of the business and affairs of the Corporation consistent with the corporate objectives.

12. Stewarded the expenditures of the Corporation and ultimately, the Corporation, within approved operating and capital budgets.

13. Established and maintained proper external and internal corporate communication to all stakeholders.

14. Abided by specific internally established control systems and authorities, led by personal example and encouraged all employees to conduct their activities within all applicable laws and the Corporation's standards and policies.

15. In conjunction with the Chief Financial Officer, provided quarterly and annual certificates as to the accuracy of the financial statements and accompanying Management's Discussion and Analysis.

16. Oversaw the monitoring and interaction by the Corporation with regard to regulatory and political matters and policy developments which may impact the Corporation either in the medium or longer term.

17. Worked with the Corporate Governance and Compensation Committees in developing appropriate succession plans and compensation structures in order to have optimum staffing to allow the achievement of the corporate goals and objectives.

As you can see, this list is largely devoid of substance; the 'goals' are the day-to-day duties of any CEO. Anyone who reads the hundreds of pages of regulatory filings can easily spot how shareholders were fed empty words in order to justify a compensation policy completely disconnected from the destruction of the value on all key per-share metrics.

A significant indicator of the market's view of Equal's management was that the company was trading at a vast discount to its net asset value—a discount as large as 60%, depending on the valuation model used. Equal also traded at a substantial discount to its peers: one metric used to value oil and gas companies is the value of each flowing barrel, which is measured by dividing the enterprise value of the company (its market capitalization plus its debt) by how many barrels it produces each day. By that measure, Equal Energy was trading at less than half the value of its directly comparable peers, and the company was equally discounted to its peers on multiple other valuation measures.

The company's discount to its net asset value, and the discount to its peers, probably had to do with the managerial failures discussed above, but there were other, broader issues. There was a flagrant problem with its corporate strategy.

Equal had previously existed as an income trust, which is a legal structure designed to provide income to shareholders. On October 31, 2006 (which, coincidentally, was the day my father died), the Canadian government eliminated that structure by a decision which came to be known as 'The Halloween Massacre' due to the consequent severe sell-off in the trust sector. Income trusts were to be phased out by January 1, 2011, and many oil and gas trusts either converted to the dividend-focused corporate structure or reverted to a growth-focused corporate structure. Equal Energy chose the latter, but it could have remained a trust. Trusts with exclusively foreign assets were allowed to remain; Equal would have had to sell its Canadian assets. It also could have become a U.S.-based Master Limited Partnership.

The Equal board's decision to become a growth-focused oil and gas company was nothing short of a disaster. Klapko made the announcement in January 2010; by early 2012, its share price had gone from around $7.00 at the time of the announcement to under $4.00. Meanwhile, per-share shareholder equity shrunk from $10.37 in 2009, to $6.35 by 2011. The growth promised by management under a corporate growth model proved illusionary, on an absolute basis, and an actual contraction on a per-share basis. As this fact became increasingly apparent, the market widened the discount between Equal's net asset value and its stock price.

From my perspective, the conversion exiled Equal Energy to No Man's Land; it was neither a growth-focused oil and gas company, nor an income vehicle. It was also neither Canadian nor American, as it lacked focus in both places. This situation, combined with a hefty debt burden, a lack of a viable strategy, and a disinterested and under-performing management team, provided no compelling reason for anyone to invest in the company, a fact reflected by the share price.

Naturally, Equal's management did not attribute the decline in the company's performance and stock price to any fault of its own. On the contrary, in my initial conversation with Equal executives, management maintained that Equal was mismanaged in the 2000s, and that it was Don Klapko who saved the company upon his hiring as a consultant in November 2007 and subsequently as CEO seven months later.

Equal certainly had encountered financial difficulties in 2006 and 2007, due to an aggressive borrowing binge by its previous CEO, Keith Conrad. But it was clear to me, what really saved the company from its over-borrowing was not Klapko as consultant or CEO—it was the unprecedented rise in energy prices. According to the U.S. Energy Information Administration, during the period from mid-2007 to mid-2008, the price of West Texas Intermediate crude jumped from $65.00/barrel to $134.00/barrel, and natural gas went from $6.00/Mcf to $11.00/Mcf. This historic rise led to a big jump in Equal's cash flow, allowing it to climb out of debt. (This period happened to correspond with Klapko's hiring as a consultant, in November 2007.) It was by no means the acumen of Klapko or his management team that saved Equal. Klapko's dismal results in the four years following his appointment proved that he was neither a visionary nor an able executive with the skills and expertise needed to tackle the challenges facing the company.

Along with the decline of shareholder equity, and per-share reserves and production during Klapko's tenure, the debt to cash flow ratio reached a higher level in 2010 than was reached under the previous "reckless" management. According to calculations based on the company's regulatory filings, the debt to cash flow ratio peaked at 4.55 in 2010, versus a previous peak of 4.32 in 2006. This is despite the fact that Equal was not paying a single penny in dividends by 2010.

Performance shortcomings aside, the company also had very poor communication with its shareholders, and with the market in general. In 2010, it stopped hosting conference calls in conjunction with its quarterly reports. Its presentations were rarely up-dated and often lacking in useful information, and its brokerage coverage was mainly limited to second-rate brokerage houses. Klapko himself was a poor communicator. He participated in only one industry conference per year and, in February 2012, made an astonishing blunder, when he publicly warned investors not to expect great results from the company's newly discovered Mississippian acreage, while he was simultaneously negotiating a joint venture to sell half of that acreage.

What made the destruction of shareholder value in Equal so hard to grasp was that it was happening in slow motion. Under Klapko's management, Equal kept a low profile, so few investors noticed that the company was slowly bleeding. The fact that most of the shareholders were retail investors with small stakes meant that management could underperform without fear of being held accountable.

As I reviewed the company results, performance and history between 2007 and 2011, I concluded that the management team was prevailing at the expense of shareholders. I decided that that was going to change, and I took it upon myself to put an end to this deteriorating performance and make Equal Energy the first target of my quest for shareholder justice.

11

WIND OF CHANGE

The future's in the air
Can feel it everywhere

The Scorpions

I invested in Equal Energy around the same time I invested in Gasfrac; both investments were initially designed to capitalize on the turmoil in the financial markets caused by the European debt crisis. I initially bought 100,000 Equal shares—not a significant investment relative to my overall portfolio at the time. Equal certainly had nothing sexy about it, but it fit with my value investing mantra, rather than with the brief renewed love affair with excessive speculation that my Gasfrac trade reflected.

By early 2012, Equal was not doing as well as I thought it should and my position was in the red. Shortly after Equal lagged, I started being hit at Gasfrac. But I had figured out what was wrong with Gasfrac: it was the slow pace of the adoption of the Gasfrac technology by the oil and gas industry. I had simply misjudged the adoptability of the technology, and there was nothing that Gasfrac's management could do to change that.

Equal seemed to be different. I looked at its assets and valuation, I researched the company and I didn't see anything wrong. There were some questions about one of its gas fields, the Hunton Field in Oklahoma—it uses a unique extraction process called 'dewatering' that produces natural gas by removing the water and then liberating the gas. My research told me, however, that this was not an issue: other companies had been dewatering since the '90s; the technology was both proven and viable.

I believed that Equal's assets were worth much more than the market was valuing them at and, by looking at other transactions in fields adjacent to where Equal was operating, I was confident the company was undervalued on an asset basis.

I concluded that Equal was salvageable and might be an opportunity to practice my nascent interest in activism. But, that understanding came a bit later; when I first invested in Equal, I was impressed enough with its potential that I published a bullish article about it on Seeking Alpha. In that article, I described Equal's attractive asset base and even praised its management for the steps it had taken to strengthen the company (eventually I found out that management had nothing to do with many of the positives I cited). That article was clearly a mistake and I soon realized I needed to further investigate the company's history, operations and management record. I did think that the positive article might have one benefit; I thought it would give me an opportunity to build some goodwill with the company. On that, I was also mistaken.

The continued fall in the share price subsequent to my initial investment signaled to me that something was wrong. As a value investor, I am highly skeptical of market efficiency and I don't always consider the market's assessment to be accurate, but this time I believed that the market was signaling something significant. I commenced an in-depth due diligence and after a few weeks of close analysis of Equal's assets, financial statements and relevant industry research reports, I found that the company was pursuing the wrong business strategy. Eventually, I realized it was both the strategy and the people behind the strategy that were the problem.

Having identified the issue, I had to figure out a way to address it; I started by writing the company a letter highlighting my concerns. On February 25, 2012, I wrote a two-page letter and faxed it to the attention of the CEO Don Klapko, and the company's chairman, Peter Carpenter. The gist of this letter was that Equal needed to change its strategy. I argued that Equal needed to reduce its debt by selling assets and again become a dividend-paying company. Alternatively, I suggested that Equal "consider strategic options".

A couple of days later, I got a call from Don Klapko and the CFO, Dell Chapman. Klapko was hostile. His tone of voice, the way he was speaking, and his whole attitude were filled with contempt, as if he was saying, "How dare you question what we're doing? Who the hell are you?" (To this point, I had said nothing publicly negative about Equal.)

Klapko actually began shouting into the phone. "You want me to sell the Hunton assets for $150 million, is that what you want?" he yelled. I replied, "I'm not asking for the company to be sold." (In my letter, I had mentioned the term 'strategic options', which often implies a sale, but I in no way implied that this should be the preferred course of action.)

Klapko's call caught me off-guard. I tried to be diplomatic. I suggested that the company revert to a trust with foreign assets. The reply was, "No, we don't have enough cash to distribute, and the yield wouldn't be high enough for an income trust." I disagreed and proposed several solutions. Then I asked Klapko about his vision, and his strategy for unlocking the company's value and turning around its fortunes. I was dumbstruck when he said, "We expect natural gas prices to rise." He was offering shareholders no added value, and apparently had no strategy to enhance the value of the company beyond waiting for natural

gas prices to rise. He made it clear that he was not ready to consider anyone's suggestion for an alternative strategy. I realized that Equal, under
his leadership, was no better than a bloated natural gas ETF (Exchange
Traded Fund) with overpaid executives who were merely waiting for the
market to change while they collected their salaries.

Chapman was much more diplomatic. He agreed that the *status quo*
could not continue and said that management understood that. It was
becoming clear that the CEO was the problem. By this time, I owned
200,000 shares, and Klapko was ignoring the fact that I was a shareholder, that I had taken the time to research and analyze the company,
and that I had some constructive ideas about how to unlock the company's value and better position it for the future.

If someone tells me 'no' in a respectful way, I'll accept it. I may not
agree, but I will certainly be more patient in dealing with it. Being disre-
spected and ignored, the way this CEO eventually ignored me, are red flags
to me. Klapko's hostility struck a nerve; perhaps his attitude reminded me
of when my father high-handedly dismissed many of my ideas. His attitude
introduced a personal element, it further motivated me to continue the fight
and confirmed that Equal was the right activism target.

I thrive in conflict situations—pressure makes me feel alive. You
would think that after having lived through many years of war, and
losing my home to it, I would shy away from conflict. But I find myself
drawn to it, and Don Klapko had just handed me a battle.

In the days and weeks following that conversation with Klapko,
I grew increasingly angry. The fact that the stock price kept falling didn't
help. More than anything, it was that discourteous conversation which
spurred me to take my activism to the next level. I wasn't sure what that
next level should be, but I knew that I would need financial resources.

At that time, Gasfrac was still holding its own, and I hoped I could
exit that position and plow my resources into Equal. I knew the most
I could buy was 5% of the outstanding shares, but this would mean

going all-in; going all-in would leave me without the resources needed to undertake a full activist battle. However, reaching the 5% threshold was key, since it would allow me to file a Schedule 13D with the U.S. Securities and Exchange Commission and give me the capacity to call a special shareholder meeting. Without at least the threat of the ability to call a special meeting, my activism would be a non-starter.

Schedule 13D is an important tool. It is a form that must be filed by anyone who acquires beneficial ownership of 5+% of any class of publicly-traded securities. A 13D filing is often used by activist shareholders as a tool to pressure management, as it signals that the share buyer is looking for corporate change. It is also helpful in expanding communication with fellow shareholders, as it alerts them to the presence of the activist and encourages supporters to declare themselves. Activists also often use the 13D as a PR tool, because letters and other communication items addressed to the board or management can be included in the filing and they become accessible to the media.

Of course, Equal's management had no idea what I was planning to do. A big part of war is perception, and they didn't know who I was, what my financial resources were, or whether or not I had any backers. I figured I could use this ignorance to my advantage.

As I contemplated concentrating my financial resources, I also knew that I was a good marketer and that I could leverage my online communication expertise to advance my cause. The combination of pouring my financial resources into Equal and backing my position with an online media campaign would telegraph to the company that shareholders were awake: 'business as usual' was over.

■ ■ ■

As a first step I needed to gain the support of Equal Energy's real owners—its shareholders. For that, I employed a dual strategy: one targeting the retail investor base, the other targeting the institutional investors. The retail shareholder base would create pressure from sheer numbers; institutional investors had clout through their access to Equal's management team, and their significant resources.

When I started my activism, 85% of the company's shares were owned by retail shareholders and 15% by institutions. Winning my battle meant winning the hearts and minds of those retail shareholders. Institutional shareholders are obliged to file ownership reports with the SEC, so they were easy to find. But the retail shareholders were dispersed throughout Canada and the United States. Reaching out to all of them would be a gigantic and expensive task.

The Internet provided part of the solution; I started an outreach campaign on the company's Internet message boards at Yahoo Finance, Investor Village and Stockhouse. I supplemented this campaign with a simple and clear online investor presentation, and through a series of articles on Seeking Alpha.

My plan worked: in a matter of weeks, I garnered the support of 50 private shareholders who held about 10% of the outstanding shares. The majority of them were small shareholders, but a few had large stakes and all pledged their support to my activist efforts.

I had already let the company know, in a letter in late February, the names and holdings of some of the people who supported my first letter; I wanted to make sure the company knew I was not just a single dissident shareholder. At that time, I had the support of shareholders holding about 500,000 shares but, by late April, that number had increased by several folds.

Convincing the institutional shareholders was another story; unlike well-known activists like Bill Ackman or Dan Loeb, I had no profile. The institutions didn't know who I was, or if I was a credible activist. I started to call them and was pleasantly surprised by the reaction; while most of the hedge fund managers were initially skeptical, they quickly changed their tune once they listened to my plans. Within a few weeks, I had enlisted the support of Equal's largest institutional investors, including Helios Capital Advisors, Breithorn Capital Management and Whetstone Capital Advisors.

Note that no Canadian firm joined the effort. It was striking how guarded the Canadian institutions were. While many expressed support privately, not one was willing to formally endorse my efforts. I remember someone representing one of the largest Canadian institutional shareholders saying, "We sympathize with your efforts, we see merits in your plans, but it is our policy not to get involved with activism." It was hard for me to understand this position: these were owners of Equal Energy, but they refused to use their rights as owners to press Equal's management team to do the right thing. If they were private shareholders I could respect their decision, but as stewards of their investors' wealth, I saw this position as a disservice to their clients. (Eventually, as natural gas prices continued to fall, the majority of Canadian institutions sold their positions and abandoned the company.)

Despite the lack of Canadian support, I managed to gather the support of institutional investors representing about 6% of the outstanding shares, or about 40% of the institutional shareholding. Then I had to decide what I was going to do with that support. I was not going to start a proxy contest. I didn't know how to start a proxy contest, and I needed to educate myself about it. I did know that it is a long and expensive endeavour so I set aside the idea as a last resort.

I decided on the simplest step: unleash the power of the shareholder base. I set out to overwhelm Equal's management with a massive campaign of letters, faxes, emails and phone calls. I spearheaded the campaign with a series of letters and articles sent to, or directed at, the company and its board of directors. At one point, I was sending a fax every 48 hours. Meanwhile, I asked the growing number of supporting retail shareholders to mount their own campaigns. I asked the institutional shareholders to use their leverage and access to the management team and directly ask them to adopt my plans, or to at least proceed with a strategic review to study viable alternatives. I wanted to bombard the management and board from all sides, and I kept thinking of the USSR's Katyusha, the much-feared multiple-rocket launcher invented by the Soviets during WWII. (The launchers were market with the factory ID 'K'; Russian soldiers nicknamed them 'Katyusha', which was the name a favourite wartime song.)

The shareholders delivered. The next two months saw both private and institutional shareholders bombarding the company with emails, letters and phone calls in support of the activist campaign.

On March 6, I sent Peter Carpenter a key letter, by registered mail, stating that my discussions with shareholders were continuing and that many institutional shareholders supported my call for "widespread change" at Equal Energy. Along with additional private shareholders, I now had over 10% of the company's owners wanting to see change at the company.

I proposed a plan for "the divestiture of the Canadian assets, and the formation of a Canadian-based dividend-paying mutual fund trust for the remaining U.S. assets, or a U.S.-based Master Limited Partnership structure." I also asked management to consider paying a dividend on the stock, to enhance its appeal to income-oriented investors and provide a way of sharing cash flow with shareholders. Income-focused energy stocks enjoy a higher valuation in the market, due to market interest in yield stocks in a severely-depressed bond yields environment, so paying a dividend would reflect well on the valuation of the company. It is important to note that a higher valuation is not just about a higher stock price for shareholders; a high valuation lowers the cost of capital for a company, and gives it a chance to grow and flourish, especially if it uses its expensive currency (shares) to acquire undervalued assets.

By this time, I realized how naïve I'd been when I wrote that positive article on Seeking Alpha. In taking the company's information at face value, and believing it was market volatility that had hit the stock price, I had missed a big piece of the story. I had assumed that Equal was well-run, that it had a strategic plan and that it would, in time, trade much closer to its net asset value.

In my subsequent articles, and in discussions with fellow shareholders, I went into in-depth detail about what I was discovering about Equal and its assets, and I made a number of strategic proposals about the direction the company should pursue. I deliberately avoided making detailed financial proposals, because I knew I did not have the full information that management had, and I did not have all the tools a CFO or a consultant/investment banker would have. I was worried that if I provided specific numbers, it would be easy for management to avoid dealing with the underlying argument for change. Poking holes in my numbers would be a distraction and would shift the discussion away from the need to have a full strategic review of the company operations, governance and positioning in the marketplace.

Recognizing that Equal was selling at a 'strategy discount', I became convinced that what the company needed was a full-scale review of its operations and plans. I was willing to offer a broad plan. First, I said Equal needed to reduce debt through the divesture of the Canadian assets, and form a joint venture for its Mississippian acreage in Oklahoma. The reduction of the company debt was a pressing concern of mine, as the company's balance sheet was not in a position to sustain a lengthy decline in oil and gas prices. Second, the company needed to be transformed into a dividend-paying entity through the formation of a Canadian-or U.S.-based trust. A trust, or Master Limited Partnership (MLP), forces management to pay out 90% of earnings to shareholders, as dividends, and it severely restricts management's ability to erode value through ill-conceived aggressive growth strategies. Despite my reservations about Equal's management, I thought a trust or MLP structure would limit the damage while simultaneously generating income for shareholders and increasing the value of the company. My suggestions were win-win, and this was a much easier activist strategy to implement because it did not require firing management or replacing board members. The implementation of this plan, however, needed to take place within the context of a full strategic review. A strategic review is a comprehensive process whereby board members, executives and, often, consultants examine and discuss an organization's position, business model and strategy for future success.

One element that both encouraged me to keep on with my activism and to further push for the transformation into a trust or MLP was the letters of support I was getting from shareholders. Some were heart-breaking; one shareholder told me that he had lost his retirement income when the company converted from a trust to a growth company. Another wrote that he'd lost his children's college funds. Both of those shareholders first bought into the company in the mid-2000s, when it was operated as a dividend-paying trust. They saw it as a safe and steady investment.

■ ■ ■

By late April 2012, Equal's share price had started to collapse and the stock hit $3.00, partially due to multi-year lows hit by natural gas and natural gas liquids (NGL) prices. Meanwhile my aggressive activist campaign was not leading to tangible results: the company was ignoring the pressure and only offering lip service about looking at "all options".

Simultaneously, my position in Gasfrac was also collapsing, as the company warned of slow sales and missed growth targets. I was at a crossroads; I had to make a decision and I had to make it quickly. If Gasfrac's share price kept falling I wouldn't have enough capital left to pursue my activism against Equal, but a significant investment in Equal would mean going all-in with a company that I knew was mismanaged, heavily leveraged and suffering from a severe decline in the value of the commodity it was selling. I weighed my options and concluded that going long on Equal was the right call. Gasfrac was clearly a bust, I was already knee-deep in my activism at Equal and I owed it to myself and to all those shareholders who believed in me to see it through. My analysis of the energy market indicated that NGL prices were due to rebound later in the year and during 2013, as the industry activated a multitude of export terminals to export the excess supply.

On April 25, I sold one million shares of Gasfrac (at a loss) and entered an order to acquire an additional 1.5 million shares of Equal Energy. It took three days to fill the Equal order, and then I promptly informed the company that I owned 4.95% of the outstanding shares. Little did anyone know that I had spent every penny I had, and borrowed some, to make it this far. Now, though, the game was on and my activism was catapulted to the next level. To that point, it had been a bluff. Now it was real, and not just to the company, but to me.

■ ■ ■

One of the key shareholders who contacted me during my activism campaign was William Cobb Hazelrig, or 'Chip', as he prefers to be called. In March 2012, Chip sent me a short email, gave me his phone number and asked me to call him. I was thrilled; Chip was a major shareholder, with about 4% of Equal's shares. I immediately called and found Chip to be pleasant; he was from Alabama and had a very charming accent. We spoke for a few minutes, and then he suggested that we speak later in the day, when his partner Fred Wedell could join the conversation.

In that conversation, Chip and Fred told me about their business background, and how they had founded Altex Energy in the late '90s (Equal Energy bought Altex in 2006). Chip and Fred were pioneers in developing the Hunton field, and they were the first backers of David Chernicky, the geologist who proposed the Hunton dewatering process. (Chernicky went on to found New Dominion, the largest Hunton private operator. He is also the Chairman of New Source Energy Partners, the first Hunton-focused MLP). Chip was also the CEO of Montclair Energy, a company he founded in 2011 to focus on drilling the Hunton formation adjacent to where Altex had operated.

Chip and Fred were friendly and approachable and we quickly developed a positive rapport. I gave them a brief summary of my background and elaborated on my plans for Equal Energy. They liked my ideas and seemed eager to see a catalyst for change emerge at Equal.

Throughout April 2012, as Equal Energy's stock dropped to new lows, I updated them on my progress. Chip raised the prospect of taking Equal private and wondered if I would be interested in joining forces with him. By late April, I already owned 4.9% of the company's outstanding shares and Chip and Fred had increased their ownership to just under 5%, so we would have been a powerful force. I respectfully declined. I didn't want to have my capital locked in a private structure and, more importantly, I felt that I would be violating my commitment to Equal shareholders. I believed I had a set of moral and professional obligations that did not jibe with taking Equal private, no matter how lucrative this proposal was.

Rejecting the idea of working privately with Chip and Fred did not chill our relationship. I felt that they would be satisfied if my activism was successful, which meant that the stock would probably double to around $6.00. And their plans to possibly proceed with a hostile offer for Equal was likely good for shareholders, as it could prove to be a catalyst for the management and the board to take corrective steps to enhance shareholder value. Chip and Fred were in a perfect win-win situation: if their bid was successful, they would own Equal for a fraction of its value; if they were unsuccessful, their bid could force the company to unlock shareholder value and increase the worth of their stake.

Their support was extremely helpful. Not only did it add credibility to my plans with other shareholders, but they had intimate knowledge about what was going on inside Equal. That became apparent in late April, when Equal's Chief Operating Officer, John Reader, resigned. Reader told Chip that he was sick of what was happening inside Equal, and that everyone in the company was tired of the pressure and the way the company was being run.

As I moved forward, I also developed relationships with a number of institutional shareholders. One of the most helpful was Jason Selch, then-portfolio manager of the energy fund operated by Helios Capital Advisors.

I contacted Jason in March 2012. At first, he sounded skeptical but, after asking me a few questions, he seemed convinced that I was serious about my goal to cause real change at Equal. He asked me to send him information about my plans, and generally expressed support for change at the company. In April, after I had increased my stake, we talked more about Equal and the path I thought it needed to pursue. Selch was adamant that the company needed to proceed with a buy-back of its shares after it sold its Canadian assets, and I told him that I wasn't opposed to this.

I was interested in Selch for another reason: he was in contact with Klapko, and he seemed to have some influence with the company. I thought it was important for him to be on board with what I saw as being in the best interest of the shareholders. Jason had access that I did not have, and through him I had some sense of what Equal's management was thinking.

■ ■ ■

154 THE BULL OF HEAVEN

While I was talking to shareholders and institutions, I continued writing to the company. The answer I usually received was that my views would be "taken under advisement", but this was not a suitable answer. The share price was crashing and the market was rapidly turning its back on Equal. In my view, the only possible solution was for there to be a publicly-announced, formal strategic review, but early on, it did not seem as if the company was prepared to undertake such a review.

Throughout March, I had written to say that a substantial number of shareholders who held a significant position in the company were dissatisfied with the company's performance. In these letters, I asked for a formal strategic review. I received only the most cursory response with the repeated statement that the company was looking at "all options".

On March 30, I sent a more forthright letter, writing that the company was making a mistake in ignoring a large part of its shareholder base. I suggested that hoping for an increase in commodity prices was not a real vision for the future. And I decided to draw a line in the sand and set a deadline of May 11, 2012 for Equal management to come up with a plan to unlock shareholder value.

My choice of May 11 was not arbitrary: it was the date of the company's Annual General Meeting in Calgary. I made it appear as if a showdown was in the cards for that meeting if the company failed to act. To increase the pressure, I contacted all of the analysts covering the company. I told them about the activist campaign and invited them to attend the AGM to witness the epic battle. I also reached out to the local press and invited many journalists.

In mid-April, Klapko called. This time, I had significant shareholder support and I could speak to him with confidence. It was a twenty-minute call, and I spoke for nineteen of those minutes. I could literally feel the rage on the other side. I pointed out that the share price was trading at $3.00 which was close to an all time low, and argued that Equal needed to immediately commence a strategic review. His only reply was: "We'll take this under advisement." While his call appeared as an attempt to appease me, his lack of engagement further worsened the situation.

Also in April, I posted three articles on Seeking Alpha: *Equal Energy vs. its Shareholders*, *Equal Energy: Excessive CEO Compensation* and *Equal Energy: Alternative Growth Plan*. Each article attracted attention and many comments. I made sure not to mince words: in my April 16 article, I flatly stated that if no action was taken before the AGM, Equal would face "an escalating shareholder revolt".

The fact that Equal had such a poor communications strategy meant that I could shape the public discourse around the company and attract attention to the issues plaguing its operations. My articles were also a way of communicating indirectly with the company's board and management.

Meanwhile, I was trying to recruit professional activist hedge funds to join my campaign. While I did have a few relationships in the investment community, none of them was in this line of business. Having no contacts has never stopped me in the past, so I gathered the names of well-known activist funds in the U.S. and Canada and started contacting them one by one.

I did not have much success until April 30, when I received a response from Peter Feld at Starboard Value, a prominent activist fund known for its involvement in the activist campaign to unlock value at AOL. Peter said that Equal was too small for Starboard, but he introduced me to David Lorber at FrontFour Capital Group, an activist firm known for its campaign to unlock value at Fisher Communications. Zachery George, son of Rick George, the legendary ex-CEO of Suncor, is one of FrontFour founders. David expressed interest in the idea and proceeded to conduct his due diligence on Equal Energy.

Then, three days after speaking with David, and eight days before the AGM, Equal announced that it would be conducting a strategic review. With that, the need to involve outside parties greatly diminished and I abandoned that effort until later in the year.

■ ■ ■

On April 26, Equal issued a news release announcing that its chairman, Peter Carpenter, was resigning (no reason was provided). He would remain on the board, and a man named Dan Botterill would become chairman. Botterill had been the CEO of Berens Energy, which he had sold for a healthy sum in 2010, after a six-week strategic review. I checked on Botterill's statements and actions at Berens; his history showed an interest in creating shareholder value.

I was eager to speak with Botterill, so I reached out to him through other members of the board. I found the contact information of two board members, Michael Doyle and Victor Dusik, and asked them to facilitate a conversation. Dusik replied, telling me that I would meet Botterill at the AGM. By that time, I was Equal's largest shareholder. I said, "No, that's not good enough. I'm the largest shareholder and it's customary that a chairman speaks to the largest shareholders when he starts his job." The next day, Dusik emailed to say that the chairman would call me that afternoon.

Dan Botterill called me on May 2, and we had a pleasant half-hour conversation. He had a soft, reassuring voice that instilled a sense of confidence and trust. I gave him the same arguments I advanced to the company in the past: the need for better governance, the need to review the company strategy, the need to reduce the debt load. Most importantly, I emphasized the need to publicly announce the start of a strategic review to halt the downward spiral in the stock price. I told him I believed this fall in the stock price could undermine the viability of the company while exposing it to a possible hostile takeover. Though Botterill refused to commit to anything specific, he seemed to be more sensitive to shareholders' concerns. I hung up the phone feeling better about the situation.

The next day, on my birthday, the company announced a strategic review. I was elated. I felt vindicated and this gave me more credibility with the shareholders who were supporting me. Most shareholders thought that I initiated this review; I later learned that other factors contributed to its initiation, but at that point, I believed the review was largely due to my efforts.

I was also relieved. I had been bluffing when I warned of serious consequences occurring at the AGM; in truth, I had no plans beyond giving a harsh speech. But the bluff was effective. Jason Selch asked what I was planning to do and said that Equal's executives were "terrified" of what could happen. I told him I didn't plan to go there with guns blazing, and likened it to watching a horror movie: people are scared of what they *imagine* is behind the door.

During that same call, Selch told me that he was having drinks with Klapko the night before the AGM, and suggested that I join them. This was very frustrating: Klapko had repeatedly refused to meet with me and I was Equal's largest shareholder, yet he was having drinks with a shareholder who had only one third of the shares I held. It seemed that Klapko was more fearful and respectful of institutional shareholders than retail shareholders, regardless of the size of their investment.

As the AGM approached, I chose to take my fiancée with me to Calgary; it was an opportunity for both of us to see a new Canadian city. We arrived in Calgary at noon on May 9 and, as we approached from the air, two things struck me: how flat the city is, and the Bow Tower. The 58-storey Bow Tower, the headquarters of the energy giants Encana and Cenovus Energy, is known as both the highest office tower in western Canada and one of the world's great skyscrapers. It is a beautiful grey glass building, with a concave arch design—and it had meaning for me, because it was built by the H&R REIT. H&R was one of the

REITs in which, as mentioned earlier, I had made one of my biggest killings. During the 2008 financial crisis, concerns about the building's cost caused H&R's shares to collapse. I bought it at just under $5.00, and sold the shares a year later for $12.00.

The cab ride from the airport showed just how different Calgary is from Vancouver. It's all business, and we rode past the massive towers of the Who's Who of the Canadian energy patch: Suncor Energy, Canadian Natural Resources, Husky Energy. You could almost smell the gas in the air; I have not felt so physically close to the oil industry since I was a kid in Baghdad.

We checked into the Fairmont Palliser, which I had chosen for its proximity to the AGM's location, and because I was meeting Jason there. At 6:00, I met Selch in the lobby—he's a thin 50-something man with a high pitched voice (and, with a unique sense of humour. In 2005, while with Bank of America, Selch protested the firing of a friend and colleague by walking into the conference room and mooning his higher-ups. He was fired, and denied $2 million in deferred compensation.)

Selch was alone. Klapko, suspecting that I would be there, did not show. So we sat in the bar and talked. Jason said that Klapko was more interested in planning for his retirement than running the business; also that Klapko didn't like controversy and I had created too much of it. We talked about various investments of interest besides Equal, and he spoke a bit about his career working for the real estate billionaire Sam Zell, and his role in the creation of Kuwait Energy.

Selch also said that he was pleased about the strategic review, and gave me credit for making it happen. He told me that he asked Klapko to drill at least three wells in the Mississippian acreage and believed that once Equal had divested its Canadian assets and further proven its Mississippian assets, it would likely be sold to an MLP. He believed that an eventual bidding war could take place between New Source Energy (which was then filing to go public), Atlas Resource Partners

(Equal's partner on some of the Mississippian acreage) and Lime Rock Resources, another MLP with Hunton exposure.

The next day, I went to the AGM, which was held in a relatively large room at the Metropolitan Centre in downtown Calgary. There were no more than 100 people present, and I was sitting alone when Dan Botterill came up and introduced himself. We had a pleasant discussion for a few minutes, and then the meeting started.

The first unusual thing I noticed was that there was no microphone for the shareholders. Then Botterill began by stating that no one could speak for more than two minutes. (My impression was that they were worried about an ambush where, in this context, a large number of shareholders surprise the board with new board nominations. If the company is not prepared, it can easily give shareholders access to board positions.)

When the formal presentations were over, a man got up to speak. I assumed that he was hired for this purpose, because he praised the CEO for the amazing job he'd done. Meanwhile, the company's shares were trading at an all-time low. It reminded me of when Saddam Hussein made speeches on Iraqi television; when he finished, someone would jump up and shower him with admiration.

I got up to speak. The strategic review had been announced, and there was no need for a speech. So I said I was pleased about the announcement and noted that shareholders were supportive of the initiative, and then I asked a technical question about the drilling plans.

After the formal session, I went to speak with Brett Undershute, the Scotia Waterous investment banker who was in charge of Equal's strategic review. Undershute is a pleasant, soft-spoken gentleman with a boyish face and thin wire glasses, like a 40-something Harry Potter. As we were talking, Klapko approached. This was the first time I had seen Don Klapko up close. He was a big man with a big belly; with my thin frame and modest height, we could not look more different.

The first thing Klapko said (and in a resentful tone) was, "You must be happy now, you will make some money!" The comment illustrated what he thought of me—he thought this whole exercise was about making a quick buck, a view that he repeated later when he described shareholders' plans as "financial engineering designed to create a quick pop," (in the stock price). The rest of our conversation was courteous. After that, I spoke to Botterill. I thanked him again for launching the strategic review and told him that I was ready to contribute whatever I could to facilitate their task. He assured me I shouldn't worry: he and Klapko would see to it that Equal's value would be realized.

12

TIME IS RUNNING OUT

I think I'm drowning
Asphyxiated
I wanna break this spell
That you've created

Muse

During the strategic review, Equal's communications slowed to a trickle. I decided to give the company time to progress. In the meantime, I offered what support I could through writing articles focused mainly on the company's assets, while highlighting its continued under-valuation.

I also started looking for ways to raise money for an eventual special shareholder meeting and a proxy contest, both of which would be necessary to force the management and board to follow shareholders' recommendations if the review failed to yield the expected results.

Equal was considered a penny stock, and having all of my capital in it did not give me access to margin borrowing. Brokers usually reduce margin lending to stocks under $5.00 and offer no lending at all for stocks under $2.00. Thus borrowing against my equity was not an option.

That left me with one choice: options. Remember that I was badly burned by options trading in 2005, so the idea made me anxious. But I had no choice—it was the only way I could generate relatively large returns with low cash outlay.

After pondering which options path to follow, I settled on selling puts against shares that had sold down sharply in the recent past. I chose this strategy because shares that decline sharply in a short period of time usually see a spike in the premium paid for the options, as the increased fear and volatility push investors and traders to buy insurance (puts) to protect themselves from further declines. I excluded from my list of potential candidates companies that had accounting problems or were operating in unpredictable and fast-moving businesses, such as technology and biotech.

My first options trade had to be a winner from the start, so I waited for the right opportunity. It came in late May, and was the options trading on the stock of the Fossil Group. Fossil Group is a worldwide fashion accessories retailer with an extensive product line. The company was doing a robust business and in April 2012, the stock was on a steady rise to over $136.00, from under $20.00 in 2009. By early May, the company warned of a slowdown in sales due to the recession in Europe, and the stock tumbled by 50% to around $70.00. I felt the decline was a massive over-reaction and opted to sell puts expiring in two weeks at $65.00; the stock hadn't seen that level in years and I expected at least a short rebound within my timeframe. The problem with short-term options is that while the risk is short-term, the premium is relatively small. So despite the massive volatility in Fossil Group shares, I had to sell $1 million face value in puts to generate $20,000 in options premiums. It was a great rate of return for a two-week commitment, but this operation had to be repeated multiple times to generate the fees I needed to fund my Equal operation. Some people would compare this type of trading to collecting pennies by jumping in front of a bulldozer; in a few weeks, that bulldozer would appear.

I wasn't sure how my broker (at that time, Bank of Montreal/BMO) would react if the Fossil Group puts were to be exercised (meaning that I had to buy $1 million worth of Fossil shares at $65.00). BMO's trading platform allowed me to initiate the trade, but I didn't know if BMO would allow me to hold the full position for an extended period. In theory, I had access to $2 million in margin allowance (at least that is what I was offered when I moved my assets to BMO a year prior), but at that time I had a boring portfolio of real estate investment trusts and blue-chip energy stocks, and not a single position in a penny energy stock. Fortunately, I didn't need to find out BMO's reaction, Fossil Group delivered.

To generate enough returns, I had to repeat the trade, so I kept scanning the market for stocks with similar characteristics. In early June, I decided to place a similar trade on another company called Tempur-Pedic, the U.S.-based mattress maker that was another Wall Street darling. Tempur-Pedic's specially-designed foam mattresses were selling like hotcakes and the stock was on a steady rise to a high of $87.00, from $10.00 two years earlier. Its stock also took a major hit after reports of slowing April sales—by May 8, it was down to $46.00. I was used to seeing this kind of volatility in commodity prices, but with a mattress-maker? I concluded that this was a perfect opportunity to place another $1 million face-value put options trade for Tempur-Pedic stock at $42.00. I placed the trade in late May with expiration in mid-June, and collected another $20,000 in additional options premiums.

My strategy of selling options to generate income was working like a charm; I placed a few other trades and, within a few weeks, I had collected over $60,000 in premiums. At this rate, I figured I would have a good war chest to initiate a special shareholder meeting should Equal's management disappoint. However, by trading in options the way I did, I was violating a cardinal rule I learned early in my career: you cannot force the market to give you what you want. I was trading with a mission to generate a specific amount of money, in a specific period, and I was taking increasing risks to achieve that goal.

On the morning of June 6, I turned on CNBC to check oil prices. In the stock ticker below, I saw that the price of another mattress-maker was down by 10%. I thought that was odd, but before I could give it another thought, I saw something unbelievable pass by the screen: TPX (Tempur-Pedic) was trading at $22.00! There had been yet another warning of slowing sales. What are the odds that a profitable mattress-maker would warn twice in six weeks, and then dive (again) by over 50%—to $22.00 from $87.00, where it was trading only few months before? But it was happening; it was real. This meant I was down over $500,000 on my options trade, I had only one week to deliver, and I doubted that BMO would advance me the money. It was nothing short of a disaster.

Where was I going to find half a million dollars on such short notice? I had to figure out a solution, and fast. I could have liquidated some of my Equal position, but that would have been a deathblow. Equal was trading at $2.75 that day with very little volume; selling 200,000 shares to raise the money would destroy the stock and take me further away from the 5% ownership threshold I needed to remain a threat to the company. My option trades usually generated $20,000 each; was there some insane options trade that would give me $500,000 in one fell swoop?

I turned to Spain. In June 2012, the European debt crisis was at its zenith, and European stocks were plunging sharper and faster than the collapse following the bankruptcy of Lehman Brother four years prior. Worse still was the state of European banks—they were joined at the hip to sovereign debt, which was where most of the damage laid.

In the midst of all of this European carnage, I figured that my salvation was going to be delivered by Banco Santander. Banco Santander was a Spanish bank, but the majority of its revenues and profits were generated outside of Spain—in Brazil, Mexico, the U.K. and the U.S. It was a conservatively-managed bank and well diversified. The bank came out of the 2008 financial crisis unscathed and its stock was trading as high as $17.00 by 2010, recovering most of the ground it lost after the Lehman crisis (it hit a low of $5.00 at the worst of the crisis). But by June 2012, with Europe imploding, the stock was again trading at $5.00, and the credit default swaps on Santander's debt were trading at a record high: the market was betting that Spain would default and would take Santander with it. All this fear also meant one thing: crazy high options premiums. So I figured the time to sell insurance was when everyone was yelling "fire".

That thinking made sense, but a Santander options trade would be tremendously risky, considering the size of the trade I had to make. The only way this trade was going to work was if the European Central Bank (ECB) was going to relent and start printing money à la the U.S. Federal Reserve. That would not happen without Germany's permission. My intuition told me that Germany was not going to allow the European Union to break, and that the ECB was going to intervene.

On June 6, I sold $3.2 million in face-value put options contracts on Santander, expiring in late September, at $7.00 a share. So if Santander's stock was not trading at $7.00 or higher by late September, I would have to come up with $3.2 million, and if Santander went bust by then (which was a possibility) I could lose $3.2 million. Such a loss would not just be the end of my activism career, as I would have to liquidate almost the entirety of my Equal position, but it would also wipe me out. Once more, I was betting it all on a single outcome, but it was a bet that netted me over $600,000 in premiums. I promptly used that amount to close the doomed Tempur-Pedic trade, and had some money left over to buy more of Equal.

Once the trade was placed, I had to wait for one of two things: either for Equal to positively conclude its strategic review, or for Santander's stock to rise above $7.00 so I could close that option trade at a profit (or for Equal to disappoint and Santander to stay at $5.00 or go lower). The waiting was hell because there was the risk of the options being exercised. When you sell puts at a price under the market price, the risk of those options being exercised is minimal, but if the stock you're selling options on is trading at $5.00 and you sell puts at $7.00, the owner can exercise that option at any time until expiration (these options are called 'American Options'). The lower the underlying stock went, the higher was the incentive for the put owner to exercise his options and put his stock to me. The other worry I had was that BMO was getting uncomfortable with my substantial options exposure. It had the power to ask me to close that trade prematurely, and that could translate into a big loss and the forced sale of some of my Equal shares.

Thus, the weeks following the Santander trade were hellish. Sleep became a memory as I followed the news from Europe on an hourly basis while constantly dreading the call from BMO informing me that the options were being exercised, or asking me to close the position. Meanwhile I had to keep my activism at Equal alive by writing articles and continuously engaging the shareholder base. I had to keep up the pretense of being confident and composed—I was anything but.

By June 26, Equal's stock had hit $2.39. By that time, my equity was barely sufficient to cover my Santander options trade. BMO started to take notice and called me a couple of times to tell me that I was in violation of their options maintenance requirements. Both times, though, they gave me a pass.

By July, I had a bit of a breather as Equal's stock stabilized and rebounded to above $3.00. But as the European debt crisis worsened, Santander took a turn for the worse.

On July 24, just before 6:00 a.m., and as Santander's stock dipped under $5.00, BMO called. My put option was being exercised. My heart stopped as I listened to the reaper announcing my execution, but I remained composed. The only words I could think of to say were, "Oh OK!" Then the broker said that the exercise would be for two contracts. Only two! I was holding thousands of contracts; two contracts was a bad joke—that was only $1400 worth of stock. My heart resumed beating.

Even though I dodged that bullet, by then, BMO was firmly on my tail, my margin allowance was reduced to $60,000, and it was pushing me to trim my options position. But two days later, ECB president Mario Draghi delivered my salvation when he pledged that he would do "whatever it takes to save the Euro." Santander rallied sharply, and I gradually trimmed my options position until I fully closed it as the stock crossed $7.00. I had snatched victory from the jaws of defeat.

With the options roller coaster over, it was time to refocus my efforts on my real battle, the Equal activist process. I also had to search for alternative methods to finance my activism—options were no longer an option.

■ ■ ■

My contact with Equal resumed in August 2012, as I wrote to Klapko and Botterill highlighting the need for the company to conclude the strategic review. The financial markets were in an agitated state due to the deterioration of the sovereign debt situation in Europe and I was worried that the situation would deteriorate further once the summer was over and Europe got back to work. Shortly after sending that email, I received an email from Klapko, thanking me for my support for the company during the strategic review process and highlighting that they were committed to finalizing the review in a proper and timely manner.

My only choice was to keep waiting, and as I waited, my relationships with shareholders continued to grow.

One of the shareholders with whom I developed a strong relationship was Dr. Adam Goldstein, who was one of the first shareholders to contact me after I started my activist campaign in February. At first, I found him annoying. He had a habit of asking multiple questions, and one answer was never enough—there was always another 'Why?' At the start, I answered all his questions, but then I got tired of it and figured that this guy was clueless; it was not up to me to educate him about the oil and gas business. Then I started to appreciate him and finally realized that he was one of the smartest people I had ever met, if not *the* smartest.

Adam's background is in technology. He had a PhD in optical communication networks and worked in Silicon Valley during the '90s tech boom, mostly as an engineer (he has multiple patents to his name). Adam is 10 years older, and we had experienced the tech boom from different vantage points—he as a participant in the technology companies of the new economy, me as a speculator in the stocks of those companies.

After the technology bust, Adam realized that his aptitude with numbers could allow him to change careers and focus on investing, where he could work from anywhere and still earn a good living. In 2006, he plunged into the markets and followed a conservative-value investing approach. He did very well, generating double-digit returns year after year and was able to leave Silicon Valley and move back to his hometown of Syracuse, NY.

As we awaited the conclusion of the strategic review, we started exchanging emails, then speaking regularly. We developed an appreciation for each other, as we spent hours talking about our investment philosophies and experience and investment ideas. We would debate our outlook for the global economy and, of course, discuss anything related to Equal. In time, we became friends.

Adam was very strong with numbers. He built elaborate spreadsheets for his key investments, and he was often more interested in the financial details of the company than the big picture of the industry where it was operating. I was the opposite—my primary interest was the industry first, then the companies operating in it. Adam was more reserved and preferred to work from behind the scenes, I was more outgoing and communicative. We saw that we could be a formidable force if we collaborated in the Equal activism. We toyed with the idea of filing a joint 13D, but we didn't share the same view on what Equal should do at the strategic review.

Although he was generally supportive of my ideas, for him, they were just ideas. He wanted to see financial models: numbers and precise calculations, not just concepts of what Equal could be. As I explained earlier, I was worried that management would shoot down any plan that was too detailed. But I started to move towards Adam's position, especially when I considered approaching other hedge funds to join my activism—most fund managers are also wired into the numbers. I realized that Adam was Equal shareholders' ace and told him, "You crack me the numbers and I will sell them to the world."

Another interesting aspect about my relationship with Adam was our different ethnic backgrounds. Adam is Jewish, and when I was growing up in Iraq, I was taught that Jews were evil people; Iraqi passports were stamped 'Valid for travel to all countries in the world except Israel'. As I grew older, I understood that the Iraqi government rhetoric about Jews was lies and propaganda. I was able to differentiate between a Jewish person and the policy of Israel (even though I was, and remain, sympathetic to the Palestinian cause and believe that the Israeli policy towards them is similar to Apartheid). Still, Adam was the first Jewish person I had ever worked with. And while he had had Arabic friends in the past, he had not worked closely with someone from Iraq. One thing that drew us closer was my understanding of the concept of being of a minority, having grown up as a Mandaean in Iraq, then living as a foreigner in France and Canada. (Later, one of our lawyers read our names on the 13D filing and declared "Peace in the World!")

We had a few disagreements; on occasion, Adam gave me the feeling of being condescended to at times (although he quickly apologized) and I'm sure that I irritated him once or twice. But what clinched our relationship was that we both had a highly ethical approach to our eventual collaboration in the Equal activism. We acted as two individuals with a fiduciary responsibility, even though we did not have that obligation. Neither one of us would entertain any notion that could somehow mislead the shareholder base, and the fact that we upheld this standard further deepened our respect for each other and underpinned our mutual trust.

By early September, four months into Equal's review process, there was no progress. I wrote to the chairman to exert some pressure, pointing out that most of the institutional investors had abandoned the company and that it was essential to deliver a review conclusion that would win back investor confidence. The chairman replied, saying that a review is a complex process, and assured me that they were continuing to work on the issues, with shareholder interests in mind "first and foremost".

I also contacted Scotia Capital's Brett Undershute, the investment banker in charge of Equal's review process. Naturally, Undershute was mum about progress, but I believed that engaging him would help him to better understand what shareholders expected. After one conversation, in which he repeated that the review process was "complex", I sensed that the review was stalling, so I wrote to the chairman again, enquiring about the nature of the complexity, while explaining that shareholders were ready to stand by him if 'complexity' was another term for internal division within the board. Botterill responded by saying that the process was on track and that the delay should ultimately prove beneficial for shareholders. On October 5, to illustrate my frustration with the lack of a conclusion, I published an article titled *Equal Energy & the Theater of the Absurd*, in which I compared the interminable wait for the review to conclude to the famous Samuel Beckett play *Waiting for Godot*.

■ ■ ■

Back when I was heavily invested in H&R REIT, I developed an affinity for dividends. The debate for and against dividend payments is a complex one. One side argues that leaving cash flow with the corporation is ultimately more beneficial, if it can be reinvested at a high rate of return. In addition, dividends are taxed twice—at the corporate level and as income for recipients. The other side argues that paying dividends is a better use of capital: it forces financial discipline on management, prevents cash hoarding, and wasteful investing in low-return projects, and provides an assured return for shareholders. Managers with impeccable capital allocation credentials, such as Warren Buffett, are rare, and investors are often better off getting their money back. As one astute investor once remarked to me, "dividends can't be restated". I believed that a dividend or income structure was the proper choice for a company with the type of slow-decline oil and gas assets Equal controlled in the Hunton formation in Oklahoma. Also, at the time, the market was awarding income energy stocks with a much higher multiple than growth stocks, thus paying a proper dividend could be the key to unlocking Equal's value. That is why, in my communications with the company and its financial advisors, I often stressed the need to initiate a meaningful dividend payment scheme at the conclusion of the strategic review.

On September 24, close to five months after the official commencement of the strategic review process, Equal Energy announced its first transaction: the sale of its Mississippian acreage and northern Hunton assets, to Atlas Resource Partners, for $40 million. The transaction was relatively small, and the press release was vague about what the company intended to do with its remaining core Hunton asset—it seemed that this asset would be retained. Without the conversion to a trust or MLP, that outcome was not of much interest to shareholders.

I feared that the strategic review was going in the wrong direction. I decided to contact some of the largest shareholders and propose that we jointly send a letter indicating what we would like to see happen at the conclusion of the review process. I wanted the letter to show the company that my views for the future of Equal were shared by several consequential shareholders, and I wanted to repeat what I had been saying since February: that we wanted to see the payment of a dividend, the formation of a trust or MLP, and the consideration of a buy-back. The letter would also indicate that if the company failed to conclude the review as expected, shareholders retained the right to work jointly or separately to challenge the legitimacy of the board (when Equal filed its 13D violation suit in January 2013, Equal quoted from this letter, but purposely omitted the word 'separately').

I wasn't sure how many shareholders were ready to endorse this letter. Several had expressed support for change, but none was working with me towards a specific goal. And while there were ninety shareholders who were supporting change, only a handful had a substantial position. I saw it fit to circulate the letter to shareholders who had at least 100,000 shares. The remaining institutional shareholders unanimously refused to endorse the letter, even if they agreed in principle with its content, and Adam refused because he disagreed with some of its requests. Still, I garnered the support of holders of 18% of the outstanding shares. I thought that my letter could not be ignored and, on October 1, I emailed it to Dan Botterill.

Ten days later, I received an official response from the chairman. He highlighted the company's progress, explained the issues and the difficulties they were dealing with and confirmed that they were considering some of our proposals. We then had a telephone conversation, in which he said that the board's consideration of the conversion of Equal into a trust or MLP was "first and foremost" (he went public with that consideration in a release issued on November 2).

On November 9, at Adam's urging, I sent Botterill another email reiterating the potential benefit of a buyback, considering that the company had a strong balance sheet since its divestures. Adam was adamant that a buyback was extremely accretive, and that it was essential for us to press the chairman to take it seriously. In this email, I also briefly discussed the potential inclusion of shareholders on the post-conversion board.

Three days later, I received what would be the last written communication from Equal's chairman. He thanked me for my support and said that all my suggestions were being considered.

■ ■ ■

During my research on Equal, and throughout my activist campaign, I had repeatedly come across the name of an energy investor who was interested in acquiring Equal. Considering her relationship with the company; I will call her 'Sarah Collins'. Sarah Collins' name was mentioned to me by at least two fund managers and one individual investor, always in the context that she was interested in Equal Energy and had made an offer to acquire the company. I also learned that she was the CEO of a private energy company, and that she was backed by a number of energy billionaires. I was told that she had worked at Goldman Sachs, and in the family offices of a number of prominent individuals. She was investment blue blood and way out of my league.

Still, I decided to seek her out. But no one would give me her contact information: she was like a valued treasure kept hidden by fund managers. Then I found her email address in an obscure online PDF. I sent her an email, introducing myself and I explained why I wanted to speak with her. To my surprise, she quickly responded and then called. She sounded young, but was very professional and cordial. We connected pretty quickly and we exchanged stories about our interest in Equal Energy.

As I spoke with Sarah, I learned that I was not the only one who was being badly treated by Don Klapko. Sarah said that she had approached the company for a deal in late 2011 and, in early 2012, made a formal offer to acquire Equal. She said that Klapko refused to deliver the offer to the board, and that she had to have some of her prominent contacts exert significant pressure to get him to deliver the offer. I do not know if Klapko ever delivered that offer. But he did deliver a masterstroke: by declaring the strategic review on May 3, 2012, he calmed rebelling shareholders and halted her efforts to acquire the company.

Sarah mentioned that Klapko was insistent that a buyout for Equal could not take place at a price below $7.00 per share, as this was around the price of Equal's 2011 secondary stock offering. It was her feeling that he didn't want to disappoint all of his friends in Calgary who had bought at that price. This $7.00 figure had also been advanced to Chip Hazelrig by Klapko, when he approached him regarding a potential buyout.

Sarah Collins naturally didn't have the same interest as Equal shareholders. Still, with her position and contacts, I felt there might be a way to work with her and that she may be able to play a key role in the activist process. I told her that if she backed our activist efforts, I could promise her that she would have a listening ear on the board. I couldn't make a commitment to a deal, but she would have a partner she could work with if a proper valuation could be agreed upon.

Sarah was initially reluctant to back our activist efforts; she was a participant in Equal's strategic review, which meant that she was bound by a confidentiality agreement that would not expire until June 2013. She also explained that, despite her differences with Klapko, she still had an open line with him (unlike the company shareholders) and she was hopeful that she could strike a deal of some sort. I highly doubted that Klapko was going to do a deal with her (ultimately, he did not).

By early 2013, Sarah reached the same conclusion I had, but she was unable to assist us in our activist campaign due to her legal restrictions. As I later learned, Klapko was very good at neutralizing and arresting threats through the intricate use of such legal tools. My experience told me that he is also someone who follows a strategy of delay in the hope that something will happen to extract him from a situation. He is like the villager in the old Middle Eastern story of The Sultan and His Donkey.

As the story goes, the sultan had a donkey and decided that he wanted the donkey to speak. He ordered his ministers to start teaching his donkey; they all explained that it could not be done. He refused to listen and told them that each would be given a month with the donkey and anyone who failed would be beheaded. A month later, he started cutting the heads off his ministers. Then he started with the teachers, professors and scientists. They all failed and he cut off their heads.

In desperation, the sultan sent his soldiers to the villages to announce that he was looking for someone to teach his donkey how to speak. Knowing that the sultan executed all who failed, no one came forward. Then one villager said, "I can teach the donkey."

The villager was taken to the sultan, and said, "I promise that I can teach your donkey how to speak, but I have the following conditions: You put me, my wife and the donkey in a castle, and provide us with food, clothing and money. You cannot speak to the donkey for ten years.

But in ten years, I promise you that he will be able to recite poetry!" The sultan, not having a better offer and having lost hope that anyone could accomplish his desire, accepted.

The villager, the wife and the donkey were put in a beautiful castle, where they lived a life of luxury. As time passed, the villager's wife started to worry—he was ignoring the donkey. She told him, "You need to start teaching it, otherwise we will die." "No one can teach this donkey how to speak," he replied. "But in ten years, either we will die, or the donkey will die, or the sultan will die!"

13

UPRISING

Rise up and take the power back,
It's time the fat cats had a heart attack,
You know that their time's coming to an end,
We have to unify and watch our flag ascend.

Muse

On the evening of November 27, 2012, I was having drinks with a friend at a Japanese restaurant. As we were chatting and drinking sake, my friend looked at his phone and said he'd just received a press release from Equal. It was after 9:00 p.m. and I thought he was kidding. But I looked and there it was; Equal had completed its strategic review.

The conclusion was stunning. In spite of multiple prior indications of a preference to convert to an income trust or MLP, the company had chosen to remain a corporation while paying a symbolic dividend. This was the first blow. Then came the bigger hit: the company had raised close to $130 million in asset sales (including the liquidation of the Canadian assets) during its seven-month review process, but instead of returning some of those funds to its owners through a buyback of its undervalued shares, or through payment of a special dividend, the board opted to hand the money back to Klapko to pursue "significant future acquisitions". The man who failed to deliver a proper growth strategy over the last five years, who had destroyed shareholder value on all key per-share metrics, and who had presided over a 75% decline in the share price since—it was to that man that the board opted to again hand shareholder wealth.

To add insult to injury, in anticipation of a shareholder revolt, the company also announced that it had retained Toronto-based Kingsdale Communications, one of the most expensive proxy solicitation firms around, and a company known for providing assistance to management teams and boards in fighting shareholder dissent.

The same press release also mentioned an interest in reviewing the board composition, and compensation polices, but those were hollow promises from a board that now lost all credibility. Equal's chairman Dan Botterill hadn't just stabbed shareholders in the back; he had twisted the dagger.

The review conclusion failed to address all of the key issues faced by the company. The strategy not only remained problematic, it was worse because Equal now had only one asset: the Hunton natural gas field, a slow-growth, slow-decline asset suitable only for the income model. The company was undervalued before the review conclusion; now that under-valuation widened against the net asset value of the company, and vis-à-vis its peers.

There were a couple of positives. The company's balance sheet was much healthier and, going forward, Equal committed to pay a twenty-cent annual dividend, so shareholders finally had a chance to share in some of their wealth, albeit at a modest level.

Comically, the release came with a meaningless graph showing how the stock had traded between the announcement of the strategic review on May 3 and November 20, days before the review's conclusion. The company asserted that the stock had traded higher prior to the conclusion and that this was a sign of confidence in Equal. Of *course* the stock traded higher during the strategic review, as the market awaited a proper conclusion. What matters is how the market *responds* to the conclusion, not what it anticipates. As expected, within a month of the review conclusion, the stock declined by 15%, thus eliminating any sign of confidence in the company.

Equal's management also proposed a worrisome budget. It was expecting $33 million in cash flow for 2013, but management was planning to spend $36 million to drill ten wells, pay $7 million in annual dividends and spend $7.5 million in general and administrative expenses. Aside from the obvious planned over-spending, it did not make sense to drill so many wells when natural gas prices were low— Equal needed to drill eight wells to keep production flat, and only six to keep reserves flat. It was clear that Equal's management was once more pushing for growth regardless of the cost, and we (Adam especially) were concerned about what the budget meant to the now-pristine balance sheet.

Having read the disaster that was the review's conclusion, I raced home and I wrote the chairman and the CEO a stern letter indicating my utter disappointment. Neither Klapko nor Botterill responded, which was surprising since Botterill and I had been writing back and forth just a few weeks earlier. I took his silence as a further indication that he had become hostile to his shareholders.

On November 28, I called Botterill at his home. I noticed a clear change: he was unquestionably annoyed. His answers were curbed and he was eager to hang up. His position became clear when he simply said, "It is what it is." He said that the board did what it felt was the best outcome for shareholders; he didn't try to explain or even pretend to care about my concerns. The call became a monologue, as I kept talking with no response on the other side. I explained that this call was our last chance to make things right, and that with no gesture from the company to rectify this review conclusion, "we will cross the Rubicon and things will get ugly." This made no difference to him.

Note that this was a public-company chairman utterly dismissing its largest shareholder. I was the owner of 1.65 million shares, or about 5% of the company shares, yet I had to plead with someone who held 0.00017% (6,000 shares). As a matter of fact, the whole Equal board collectively held a mere 1.3% of the outstanding stock (shares which were mostly granted, not acquired), yet this group of economic tourists controlled the fate of thousands of real owners.

The next morning, Adam called Botterill to try to reason with him. He also got the cold shoulder, but he was able to ask why the company had hired Kingsdale. At first, Botterill said it was to improve communication with shareholders but, when pressed, he admitted that it was because Equal had a group of hostile shareholders, hence the need to protect the company. I certainly did not consider my relationship with Botterill to be hostile; evidently, he did.

On November 29, once it was clear that the company was unwilling to budge, Adam and I issued our first official press release. We were not the only ones who disapproved of the strategic review's conclusions: a large number of shareholders were already voicing their discontent with calls and emails to Equal, and through messages on the online forums. In our press release, we attempted to capture this shareholder frustration, and we recommended that the company take a number of steps to rectify the situation. Those recommendations eventually became our 'Five-Point Plan', which called for:

1.   An immediate halt to excessive capital spending and the pursuit of acquisitions; and a focus on returning cash to shareholders,

2. The initiation of a substantial share buyback through open-market operations, or through a Dutch auction at a maximum price of $3.75 per share. (In a Dutch auction, the price is set after bidding; in a buyback, the reverse occurs and shareholders tender to the company.)

3. A material increase in the amount of the annual dividend,

4. The introduction of shareholder representatives on the board of directors,

5. The resumption of the strategic review process to further explore alternatives to enhance shareholder value, including the possibility of restructuring into a trust or MLP.

The plan was anathema to Equal's management. We believe that they read the points as:

1. No growth,

2. Less capital for growth,

3. Less cash flow for growth,

4. Oversight to restrict business and compensation growth,

5. A legal structure that would limit growth.

As my investment career evolved and I developed a deeper understanding of companies and the underlying motivations of management teams, I was struck by the obsession with growth. It's an obsession held by CEOs, investors, bankers, politicians, economists and nations—humans are wired to grow. But growth can also be problematic; in the corporate context, companies that adopt aggressive growth strategies can find themselves overextended, losing money and out of business.

At Equal, growth was one of the core issues of dispute. Management was fixated on growing the company at any cost; this was the underlying driver for Equal's 2010 conversion from a trust into a growth-focused oil and gas company. Growth can be very beneficial when executed correctly, but in the case of Equal, it was not.

Our Five-Point Plan was designed to halt further questionable growth. Growth could resume when the company value was unlocked, and it could be undertaken on a per-share basis. But when a CEO has a grandiose vision of building the next Standard Oil, those five points were of no interest, regardless of their likely positive impact on the share price or his shareholders' investment.

The issue of returning capital to shareholders is a touchy subject for many CEOs; once a manager has capital, he usually doesn't want to part with it. It was the same when my father was in the Ministry of Industry in Baghdad; division managers were hesitant to return unspent funds to the treasury, fearing it would reduce their allocation in the next calendar year. CEOs are no different: a dividend once established is hard to retract, and once funds are spent on a buyback, they can't be invested in the business.

A manager will argue that the funds are better being reinvested in growing and developing the business. In the energy business, that assertion can easily be manipulated to reflect a certain outcome. For example, an oil or gas well often produces hydrocarbons for twenty years. The expected return on that well can be over-estimated by adopting an optimistic outlook for oil prices over that period. That justifies spending money on drilling: more wells, more reserves, more production. And if an executive is manipulative, he can state that increased production on an absolute basis, rather than a per-share basis, and cloud the picture for investors.

One complicating factor in the Equal situation was that Don Klapko was, by training, a facilities engineer. As such, he seemed to lack a proper understanding of the multitude of parameters governing the management of a publicly-traded company. I remember an incident recounted to me by a U.S. fund manager who met with Klapko. Every time he asked a financial question, Klapko referred it to his CFO; he was clearly uncomfortable addressing issues not pertaining to the operation of an oil or gas field. I always believed that Klapko should have been hired as a Chief Operating Officer, rather than a Chief Executive Officer; that fund manager agreed.

Klapko is not exceptional in his refusal to admit failing to create shareholder value; most executives are loath to admit such failure and thus resist returning capital to shareholders. It's not just an ego problem; it can be seen as an actual conflict of interest, as this failure can lead to a CEO's dismissal. It could be argued that it falls into the definition of the classic Agency Problem (or the Principal-Agent Problem), where the agent fails in a duty to make decisions that would best serve the principal; and that that failure stems from self-interest, which is inherently a conflict of interest. This problem has been debated in academia and the business community for decades, and a number of safeguards are in place to deal with it. Boards of directors are supposed to be one safeguard, but as we have seen at Equal, boards can be part of the problem.

■ ■ ■

On December 3, in response to our press release, Equal fired back with its own press release. It was a stunning personal attack, with Equal's management attempting to belittle and denigrate Adam and me. The release portrayed us as two clueless bloggers who were promoting a reckless and unsuitable strategy for Equal, a strategy designed to benefit a minority of shareholders. The release confirmed my long-held suspicions about Klapko's position; what was distressing was the 180-degree flip by Botterill, as it confirmed that nobody on Equal's board was actually working for the benefit of its shareholders.

Once we saw what we were dealing with, Adam and I decided to jointly file a 13D. We also launched a dissident website, www.SaveEqualEnergy. com. Our website was fully loaded with analysis, plans, slides, graphs, videos and links to the many articles we had published about the company over the preceding months. We also hosted a forum where shareholders could meet and debate solutions to the Equal problem. The decision to file a 13D and the launch of the website greatly enhanced the profile of our cause; our activism became an outright revolution.

Even though we were pursuing an escalating media campaign, and despite being denigrated and belittled by the company, we still hoped that the matter could be amicably resolved. Throughout the month of December, we pleaded with the company to meet with shareholders, and a number of shareholders attempted to mediate, but the company categorically refused to meet with us. In one of our 'begging emails', which is what Adam came to call them, I quoted Abraham Lincoln's assertion that "a house divided against itself cannot stand" and I strongly urged them to reconsider their position.

We were trying to avoid resorting to a proxy contest, not just because it's a complicated and expensive undertaking, but also because we genuinely believed that an escalating public fight was not in the best interest of the company and its shareholders. Such a battle would not only drain everyone's resources, it would also be an invitation for hostile entities to capitalize on the conflict.

Unfortunately, the more Equal's management refused to engage with us, the more compelled we felt to take further public action to pressure them to deal with shareholders. On December 13, Adam and I filed the 13D. This was a demonstration of force; to that point, the company may have thought we were bluffing. Attached to the filing was a letter to the board in which we stated the issues we saw as problematic and offered our Five-Point Plan as a solution. Shortly after the filing, I sent an email to Michael Doyle, head of Equal's nomination and governance committee, reiterating our demands and proposing that shareholders be considered for nomination to the board of directors. The company had publicly alluded to an interest in reviewing the composition of the board; this was its chance to demonstrate sincerity. I gave Doyle until December 20 to respond; on that day, I received an email from Kingsdale representative Bernard Simon, who said that Equal was ready to consider shareholder board nominations, if we could submit them by January 18. This was encouraging. Not only was our proposal being considered, but Simon had previously refused to speak with us. In fact, I had called him earlier, to signal an error with a company presentation, and took the opportunity to suggest that they enter into talks with us about the outstanding issues between the company and its shareholders—he hung up on me.

It did occur to us that the company was just playing for time; if we were going to submit shareholder proposals or commence a proxy contest, we needed to do so by February 8. So we sent the company details about our board nominations and gave it until January 11 to respond. We also promised to cease public pressure until that date.

The company did not reciprocate. The next day, Equal posted a video on its website, attacking us yet again. In the video, it was suggested that our plan was a form of financial engineering designed to "orchestrate a short-term pop", and meant to take Equal back to the dark days of over-leverage (a curious accusation given that I had long been pressuring the board to reduce debt). Once that video was posted, we realized that the company was not dealing in good faith and chose to resume our pressure.

It was sad to see the company wasting money on video productions and attacks designed to fight shareholders—it could have held a conference call, as was customary. Instead, this tactic backfired as we quickly uploaded the video to our website and added sub-titles refuting and discrediting all of Klapko's assertions. Within days, our viewership exceeded Equal's by a factor of 3 to 1.

Equal's hiring of Kingsdale was a major mistake. First, Kingsdale's ethics appeared to be questionable. Before the strategic review was concluded, and at the urging of a shareholder, I called Kingsdale to ask about the possibility of a collaboration if Equal failed to deliver a proper conclusion to the review. Kingsdale's general counsel, Roop Mundi, quickly organized a conference call, which included one of his Toronto-based colleagues. In that call, they tried very hard to sell me on their services, and then followed up with a detailed proposal. Mundi, who was based in Vancouver, also proposed that we meet for coffee, but I declined. I got the sense that Kingsdale was interested in inflaming a conflict with Equal, not solving it.

Sure enough, when Equal released its review conclusions, there was Kingsdale's name on the press release. We don't know if Kingsdale was already in talks with Equal, if it approached Equal because it smelled a lucrative client or if, by coincidence, Equal contacted Kingsdale. Regardless, once Kingsdale was retained by Equal, Mundi ceased to acknowledge my emails. Kingsdale had shown itself to be willing to back any party as long as it got paid, and I made it clear to Equal's board that hiring mercenaries to fight shareholders was the wrong strategy—and a further waste of shareholder capital. Note that the fee that Kingsdale quoted in its proposal to me (excluding communication expenses) was $225,000, including a $100,000 success fee.

Equal's attitude towards paying consulting fees demonstrated the same attitude to managing the company: spend and over-spend, hire the most expensive proxy solicitation firm, hire the most expensive law firm. While executives were collecting multi-million dollar salaries, and paying outsiders huge fees, they didn't care that it wasn't their money to spend.

With the huge contrast between what resources were available to Equal and what were available to shareholders, costs were becoming a problem. We had to be creative, so we focused on viral marketing. Successful viral marketing requires content that is original, informative and entertaining, and we strove to achieve that. As we saw the company's rigid refusal to negotiate with us as childish, we conducted a Lollipop campaign, in which we asked each shareholder to mail seven lollipops to the board (one lollipop for each director). Equal's Calgary office was flooded with lollipops. We also produced videos: one explained our Five-Point Plan through two talking teddy bears, another was a re-make of an Internet parody of Hitler in the German movie *The Fall;* in our version, Klapko was portrayed as Hitler hiding in his bunker as shareholders advanced, with his board and Kingsdale failing to halt their progress. YouTube, popular finance blog websites and social media sites gave us the scope we needed to fight back. We knew how to use the Internet; Equal was far behind in this respect. The situation was similar to a traditional army using tanks and airplanes in battle against an agile and lethal urban insurgency. If a corporation wants to fight tech-savvy shareholders, it has to be equally savvy—or its consultants have to be, and Kingsdale did not seem up to the task.

An activism project is not a sprint: it's a marathon. You need to keep moving forward at a steady pace; I call it "life compounding". Compounding your actions over a long period can prove to be a formidable force. During those charged activism days, I started every morning with a plan to accomplish at least one task. Every day I called share-holders, sought out new supporting activists, emailed or called Equal, interacted with shareholders on online forums, and prospected for both proxy solicitation firms and board members. I wrote articles, worked on slides and videos, coordinated information on the dissident website, worked on a preliminary information circular, and researched additional relevant information about the company and its assets. I issued press releases, strategized with partners and supporters, posted on social networks, spoke with legal counsel and managed finances to locate enough funding for the duration of the campaign.

That seems like a lot but when done one step at a time; it is much more manageable than it sounds. There were intense periods of heavy work, but I paced myself. What I lacked in terms of human resources, I made up with commitment. One key advantage of conducting the activism with my own funds was that I had no deadline pressure from clients.

This is how I visually represented the pressure of the activism campaign on the company:

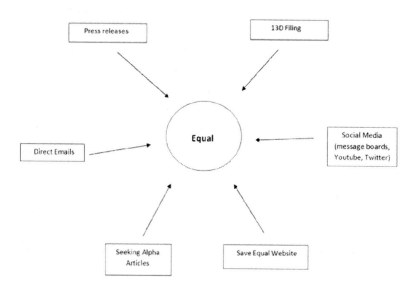

If the need had arisen, we had further plans. As part of a proxy contest, we were prepared to raise the money needed for a full advertising campaign, and budget for radio and newspaper ads to run in conjunction with the filing of a dissident circular (which usually costs about $150,000). We were prepared to commission research reports, and solicit coverage from the mainstream media. We were prepared to encourage large-scale investors to bid on the company, and we were prepared to formally request the full shareholder list and contact all shareholders to exhort them to assert direct pressure. In other words, we were prepared to go all the way.

In the Middle East, there is a saying: 'Nagging can undo welded metal'. In other words, if you keep pushing a little every day, you will be able to break anything. The Chinese learned that a long time ago, hence the invention of water torture. That is how I pictured my pressure on Equal's board. After the 2013 shareholder meeting, Botterill said he would never again serve as a director of a public company—after enduring the pressure of our campaign. He was both blaming shareholders and crediting them for his resignation. It didn't have to be that way—he could have simply listened to the owners of the company.

Our campaign was effective, but we were running low on funds. We were spending thousands on press releases, and the early talks with lawyers about a proxy contest were starting to bite. BMO had cut my margin loan power to $60,000, I was fully invested in Equal and my personal credit lines were maxed. Financing a proxy contest would cost at least $500,000, not counting litigation fees—we would get most of any proxy contest fees back if we won, but we first had to come up with the cash. The only way to solve that problem was to find a brokerage firm that would advance money against my capital. But the Canadian banking system is almost an oligopoly: if one refuses you, the rest will follow suit. As we were contemplating this problem, Equal hit us, and hit us hard.

14

IN THE ARMY NOW

Shots ring out in the dead of night
The sergeant calls 'Stand up and fight!

Status Quo

On January 24, 2013, after a long period of silence and refusal to engage with its shareholders, Equal Energy filed a wide-ranging lawsuit in New York's 13th District Court against me, Adam and 250 John Does. The lawsuit alleged violation of SEC 13D filing regulations and 14A proxy solicitations. Equal did not have the decency to inform us directly before making the suit public; I learned of it in a press release. In addition, in a striking example of how these people operate, they requested an expedited hearing—for 2:00 p.m. the following afternoon, in New York, meaning that we had that small amount of time to find legal representation.

The speed and the magnitude of the lawsuit were designed to overwhelm us. The company's position was also confusing: just a few weeks earlier, Adam and I were portrayed as a couple of ignorant dissidents—now we were a clear and present danger that had to be immediately dealt with, regardless of the cost to shareholders.

I can't say I was that surprised. I thought that management would try to sue us at some point, but certainly only after all diplomacy had been exhausted. In its press release of December 3, Equal twice referred to its 'fiduciary duty'; if that duty mattered to the board, it would have actually communicated with us, rather than wasted shareholder funds on an expensive and unnecessary lawsuit. Kingsdale's contribution may have also been at play, since a friendly resolution to the conflict was not necessarily in their best interest.

The lawsuit could not have come at a worse time. My financial resources were running dangerously low and, hours before the company filed its lawsuit, BMO informed me that it would not be increasing my personal credit line. I therefore did not have the funds to initiate a proxy contest and I certainly did not have the funds to fight a lawsuit.

The suit was largely devoid of merit. It was also sloppily prepared. Many of the accusations were invented. For example, Equal claimed that, as part of my conspiracy against the company, I traveled to New York to meet with hedge fund managers—I have never been to New York. Still, a judge decided that there was enough substance to allow it to proceed. This was largely due to a series of errors Adam and I had committed early in the campaign. For example, we had made the public assertion that we had between 10% and 30% shareholder support (subsequent voting showed that we had under-estimated the amount of support). Unfortunately, disclosing our level of support publicly, gave the company the fodder it needed to launch its lawsuit.

The lawsuit focused mainly on the content of our 13D filing, specifically whether it was sufficiently descriptive of the extent of our fellow shareholders support. The 13D filing regulation is case-specific and there is no clear-cut test to qualify whether the support we had was sufficient to be included in a 13D. In order for the judge to decide if we were in breach of the 13D regulation, we had to provide her with our record of communication with shareholders: that was over 7,000 emails. This was a red line for me. Aside from violating the trust and privacy of my fellow shareholders, having a lawyer go through all of those emails would entail a tremendous financial cost. In addition, that email record included conversations with people who I believed were bound by non-disclosure agreements with Equal. Some of those people had an interest in acquiring Equal; others had had disputes with management. Regardless of why they had signed their agreements, disclosing their identities would have caused them irreparable harm.

As it happened, I had anticipated needing a lawyer to help us prepare for the possibility of a special shareholder meeting, and I had recently hired Gary Gill at Vancouver's Sangra Moller LLP. Sangra Moller is a boutique law firm, but its experience in activism was well known and I knew that Gary could be helpful in guiding us through a proxy contest.

Fortunately, Gary had a relationship with the New York firm of Kleinberg, Kaplan, Wolff & Cohen. Unfortunately, securities attorneys do not come cheap; the retainer alone was $25,000 and that was just to have them represent us the next day. I had $15,000 left on my line of credit and convinced Adam to pay $10,000. Then I had to scramble to find a solution.

Selling Equal stock to fund the litigation was not an option, as doing so would have killed our chances of mounting a proxy contest. If my ownership with Adam dipped under 5%, we would be prevented from initiating a special shareholder meeting, and selling shares would signal to the company that we were not in a position to fight.

Still, with funds running low and the pressure of the lawsuit mounting, I had to make a choice: fight, delay or surrender. For the first time in that long battle, the thought of surrender crossed my mind. In the first conference call we had with our New York firm (a long-distance meeting with five attorneys each billing up to $800.00 an hour), our lead lawyer, David Levy, asked us, "What do you have in mind? How do you want to play this?" I replied, "I am a French citizen. My first thought is 'surrender'." Everyone had a good laugh, but I was only half kidding.

During the early days of the lawsuit, I worked frantically with our lawyers to contain the situation. With the accelerated schedule that Equal had obtained by claiming imminent threat, the lawsuit would be wrapped up in a couple of months. But with that pace came massive legal fees: $33,000 in the first week alone. Adam even considered defending himself, but our lawyers quickly talked him out of it, with attorney Chris Davis calling it "suicide".

One day in the early morning of February 2013, as I was battling this giant of a corporation, I was standing at my window, watching people heading to work in the rain. I turned my head to the cloudy sky and had the feeling of literally punching at the stratosphere. Suddenly, I felt a world apart from my comfort zone and it excited and terrified me.

We all have moments when we have to make decisions that can demolish or build our futures, and the futures of those around us. I realized that this was one of those moments. I thought of leaders we revere—Napoleon, Alexander the Great, Genghis Khan. I wondered how those men felt as they made decisions that not only shaped their own personal histories, but also the histories of their nations and the history of the world. How did they know how far to go? How did they know when to stop? When you have absolute power, the only barrier to your actions is your imagination and the physical limitations of your nation. Those men lived on the edge. They had no one to lean on— everyone was leaning on them. It is a scary thought when the road ahead is the vastness of the universe and there are no signs to go by; I had nothing to point me in the right direction.

With my options limited, I even considered ignoring the court altogether. I was a French citizen residing in Canada and did not consider myself answerable to the New York District Court. But refusing to

acknowledge the suit would leave Adam to shoulder the burden alone—
plus, Equal could launch a similar action in Canada.

One problem I had was that I was paying 93% of the legal fees (it
was proportional to our respective ownership in the company). This was
how Adam and I structured our arrangement when we filed our 13D; it
was only a verbal agreement, but I had to honour it.

My word has always meant a lot to me. When I was seven years
old, my father took me with him in a car ride to the edge of Baghdad,
where we stopped at a farm (it was the first time I saw someone milking
a cow). Then my father walked towards a half-built structure partially
covered by a tent. We sat on the floor (traditional Arabic living rooms
don't have sofas) and he spoke with a group of men who dressed in classic Arabic attire. Father pulled stacks of dinars from his briefcase, they
all shook hands, then they served us tea and we left. Later, my father
said that he had just purchased the farm. Even at that age, I knew that
people needed to sign contracts to buy land. When I asked him about
it, he said, "Son, those simple people abide by a Bedouin culture; their
word is their bond. We will sign the papers later, but as of now the land
is ours." I was fascinated to see that you could give someone so much
money with only the trust of his word and a handshake. I have never
forgotten this experience and when I give my word, I work hard to honour it. I don't believe I've maintained a perfect record, but I've done my
best and am proud of it.

My only option with the Equal suit was to find the money to fight
it. It's not that I was broke; my balance sheet was very strong and my
Equal stake was worth over $5 million. My problem was that I didn't
have liquidity, and I had to find someone to lend me $500,000 using
my Equal stock as collateral. I therefore commenced a frantic search for
an amenable brokerage house. The big Canadian banks were hopeless;
I knew that if BMO was not willing to lend me the money, the others

would also refuse. I had dealt with other large Canadian banks in the past: TD Canada Trust, which was even more conservative than BMO; and the Royal Bank of Canada, which had offered me very limited margin flexibility when I once considered moving my assets there. The only real chance I had was with the smaller brokerage firms and I went through about a dozen before finding a Toronto-based brokerage that was ready to advance me the money. I was so relieved at finally having room to maneuver, I didn't even ask them how much interest they were going to charge.

Once I'd told my lawyers that we didn't need to surrender, we proceeded on two simultaneous paths: we considered ways of having the lawsuit dismissed, while actively fighting it. Our strategy consisted of demonstrating to the judge that we were not planning to initiate a special shareholder meeting or take control of the company, while in our communications with the company we retained that option. Equal had filed its lawsuit too early, i.e. it was filed before Adam and I had requested a special shareholder meeting, or taken other official measures to challenge the board such as filing a shareholder proposal to be included in the 2013 circular. We decided to capitalize on that. We updated our 13D filing in early February, expressing our new position of taking no official action against the company at or before the next shareholder meeting. This stance would delay our action to later in the year, but it would also pull the rug out from the company's premise that we presented an urgent danger; hence the suit could be delayed or dismissed.

In mid-February, Equal responded to our updated filing by dropping the 14A proxy solicitation charge, but it maintained the 13D violation allegation. They also added to the list of accusations, many of which were simply based on 'information and belief' which, in plain language, means 'we have no proof, so we are guessing or making it up'.

Following this response, lawyers for both sides met in the presence of the judge to see if an amicable solution could be found. According to our attorney, the judge seemed annoyed with the company's aggressive stance; we had backed down, so it was unclear why they were pressing to continue with the suit on an accelerated schedule. Equal's lawyers argued that our activities were hampering the search for new directors (we had learned that the company was planning to replace some of its directors; three new directors were handpicked, with the legacy directors retaining majority positions).

Equal also claimed that our 13D filing was deficient, saying that our disclosed 5% ownership did not reflect the true extent of ownership supporting our position. This goes back to our error of stating that we had 10% to 30% support—Equal argued that those shareholders should have been included in the 13D filing (even though the type of support we had did not require us to include those people, nor could we have included them against their wishes). The company pressed for more disclosure and more updates to the 13D filing with details on our supporting shareholders, contacts, plans and activities—note that they did not know who the John Does were.

The judge asked both parties to work to arrive at a mutually-acceptable language for an updated 13D filing. While this was a reasonable solution, we suspected that no amount of updates to the filing would satisfy the company, as with each disclosure the company could claim it was not sufficient. This process could go on for a long time, draining us of funds and energy, and the discovery process regarding the email record was still in effect.

This whole situation reminded me of the search for Weapons of Mass Destruction in Iraq. As you'll recall, in the lead-up to the 2003 American invasion of Iraq, the Bush administration maintained that Iraq was hiding Weapons of Mass Destruction. Every time a UN inspection failed to find WMDs, the U.S. administration maintained that WMDs were there. But it is not possible to prove a negative—according to our lawyers, we had no 13D group within the meaning of 13D regulations.

It was just me and Adam as we indicated in our 13D filing, but it was impossible to prove that with mere 13D updates. Equal was on the hunt for our anti-Equal WMDs and was determined to invade us to find them. Our fighting strategy was failing.

At the same time, Adam was pursuing a settlement, but Equal would not settle with one of us. It wanted both of us to settle and that again left Adam in a precarious situation, since he was not able to claim jurisdiction as a basis for dismissal of the suit. I opted to consider a settlement, on one condition: I would not hand over any of the communication that had taken place with shareholders, or any other parties. If the company insisted, I was ready to 'go rogue' and continue my campaign in Canada.

Thankfully, the company did not insist. It did, however, present us with a horrendous settlement offer. This offer contained an obligation to vote for Klapko and the company directors, a thirty-month standstill period, and an allowance for Equal to retain the option of launching a separate defamation action. Equal's management also demanded that we remove all online material against the company and cease all activist efforts. The last two requests were workable, but the rest was totally unacceptable, especially the demand to vote for Klapko. I remember telling my lawyer "I'd rather drink poison than vote for Klapko." A man who had caused so much harm to me, and to so many shareholders and their families, was not going to get my vote.

Adam and I maintained that position through most of February. The company did not budge, but time was passing and the discovery process was becoming tedious. Equal's lawyers wanted to know about everyone with whom we ever discussed Equal, shareholders or not. They wanted to learn about every letter, every plan, every piece of communication—pretty much every thought we had ever had about the company since January 2012. Gathering all of that information was a mammoth task. I did my best to stall but Adam was not ready to defy the judge, and that was a source of worry to me.

In late February, we got a break. After a meeting between David Levy and the Equal lawyers, the company changed its tune and dropped its demand that we vote for the management and directors. It also cut the standstill period to fifteen months and dropped its option of filing a defamation suit. Equal also bowed to my key demand by dropping the requirement to divulge our communications with shareholders or other parties, which meant that their identities would remain protected.

The terms of the standstill were definitely lop-sided: Adam and I were not allowed to challenge Equal's board or management. We were to have no communication with other shareholders and had to agree to undertake no legal action. Equal simply agreed to take no legal action against us and was allowed to continue with business as usual.

We signed a standstill agreement on March 19 and the lawsuit was dropped few days later. We later learned why the company changed tracks so quickly: on February 25, Chip Hazelrig and Fred Waddell at Montclair Energy had approached Equal with a takeover offer. Equal, possibly fearing a possible hostile process, had to dispense with Adam and me.

The Equal lawsuit demonstrates how companies can manipulate the legal system to squelch dissent. A company does not need to prove a wrongdoing; it just needs to introduce enough suggestion that a wrong has been committed. This pulls shareholders into an expensive legal process, where the shareholders pay from their pockets and the company pays with shareholder money. Winning that lawsuit against Equal would have cost us at least $500,000 and it would have changed nothing—the management team and board would still be in charge and we would still have to go through a proxy contest. Equal could also have filed new suits—when money is no object, death by a thousand cuts becomes death by a thousand lawsuits.

The activism process cost me $200,000, with most of that going to legal fees. Equal's management never revealed what it had spent in its fight against shareholders, choosing to bundle fees under 'administrative expenses'. I did make enquiries though. Based on anecdotal evidence gathered from people close to the company, I estimate that Equal spent between $2 million and $3 million on lawyers and PR firms to fight its shareholders—using shareholder money. To put that into context, the company's annual dividend cost $7 million; if it hadn't wasted shareholder capital on an unnecessary lawsuit, the 2013 dividend would have been 28% to 42% higher.

The settlement certainly put a halt to my activist process, but it also put Adam and me on the map. Prior to the lawsuit, many of the activist funds we approached didn't take us seriously. It was Equal's launch of the suit against us that proved we were the real thing.

15

THE SHOW MUST GO ON

My soul is painted like the wings of butterflies
Fairy tales of yesterday will grow but never die

Queen

Equal Energy's leadership portrayed my activism as "financial engineering designed to cause a short-term pop", but my battle was never motivated by greed. It was driven by a profound sense of injustice at the wrongs committed against the company's shareholders. I had listened to shareholders tell me about losing their savings and children's education funds due to mismanagement and lack of proper oversight. That hardened my resolve to engage in the battle to hold the company executives accountable, and to demand dividend payments and measures to strengthen the company and enhance its value. If Equal's management had taken the time to meet with me, they would have seen that.

Personal behaviour is often defined by how we mentally frame a certain activity. If I had framed my activism as being driven by profit, I doubt that I would have persisted. But framing my struggle as a battle between good and evil completely changed the nature of my involvement. Suddenly, I wasn't just another financial activist; I was a modern-day Robin Hood, taking from the oppressors and giving to those who had been wronged.

It is hard to say why I framed my activism in this manner. Perhaps I was searching for meaning in my life; perhaps it was just idealism about what is right and what is wrong. While I have spent much of my life chasing wealth, I knew that life is most meaningful when it transcends the material and moves into the realm of love, friendship, altruism and the search for knowledge. I lived my childhood where we had real-life war heroes: I vividly remember the statue of the Iraqi pilot who, when he ran out of ammunition, flew his plane directly into an Iranian bomber headed for Baghdad. Now, I felt I was becoming that hero, sacrificing everything for a just cause.

To engage in a conflict with an entity that is many times larger requires an extreme level of conviction, because at the darkest hour, that conviction is the only thing you will be able to hang onto. During my activism, there were times when every fibre of my being urged me to stop. What kept me going was my knowledge that my cause was just and that, if successful, I would positively influence the life of thousands of people.

One of the most effective ways to scare shareholders is to threaten to drain them of money. But if you're going to engage in a battle that transcends money, you need to unshackle yourself of the fear of losing it. Money is a means to an end, not an end in itself. This disregard for the financial cost of the Equal battle was the key to my survival. I figured early on that money would not be a deciding factor; while generating a sizable profit from my activism would be exciting, the real value was in righting a wrong and holding accountable those who had sinned.

War has its own form of romanticism, and soldiers long for the feeling of camaraderie, solidarity and sacrifice that war brings. I spent the entirety of my childhood exposed to the horrors and destruction of war, but also to the love and unity it unlocks between families, friends and communities. I still hunger for that common sense of purpose and destiny and, in its own way, my battle with Equal offered that feeling.

My settlement was purely a tactical retreat. My cause was just and I wasn't going to completely surrender to what I perceived to be the power of greed and avarice. So once it was signed, and while waiting for the standstill to expire, I prepared for a prolonged guerrilla war against the company. Some may see this as unethical but, as far as I was concerned, Equal had been dealing in bad faith from the beginning; the settlement was just another move in the game.

It was vital that I maintain contact with key shareholders, and I stayed in touch with Chip Hazelrig, Andrew Shapiro and another fund manager who prefers to remain anonymous. Collectively, they owned 12% of the company. With my stake, I believed that 17% was consequential enough to keep engaged until the standstill period expired. A handful of private shareholders also maintained contact with me, but I made sure that my conversations with them did not violate the terms of the settlement. My relationship with Adam continued as before, and even strengthened after persisting together and surviving Equal's attack.

My guerilla strategy had three goals: to maintain the pressure against the company indirectly through feeding shareholders my arguments; to encourage Chip Hazelrig to bid for the company, thus forcing it to change course, and to possibly find a white knight. While I had previously been opposed to the company being sold, I found that the idea was growing on me—if the price was right.

In early January, Chip and Fred called me to ask about Equal's business, legal structure and shareholder composition. Their questions signaled an interest in making a bid for Equal through their company Montclair Energy. I informed them that I was ready to share information, while reiterating my stance from a year earlier that I wasn't interested in joining a bid myself.

In March, a few days after signing the settlement agreement, I received a call from Debt Advisor's Randy Lampert, the investment banker hired by Montclair to prepare a bid for Equal. Randy asked if I was interested in selling my Equal shares to Chip, and said he was willing to give me a one-year option to recover any capital gains I might miss if a transaction took place during the standstill period. I quickly turned down the proposal, I felt that such action would probably flagrantly violate my settlement agreement. Furthermore, I would have had to update my 13D filing, which would alert the company to the transaction. I was also in no hurry to part with shares that had started to pay me a quarterly dividend that I had fought so hard for.

On March 25, Montclair Energy publicly announced its intention to bid $4.00 a share for Equal. It was a lowball bid, but I was glad that Chip and Fred had pulled the trigger; it was vital that shareholders maintain active pressure now that I was sidelined. The prospect of a hostile bid was not going to sit well with Equal's board and management. I made sure that the media was aware of Montclair's potential bid and, using a pseudonym, notified BNN's Jameson Berkow—Once alerted, I gathered that BNN would keep referring back to the story every time a development took place. Berkow did a live segment on Equal and wrote a detailed blog post on BNN's website.

Equal's board acknowledged Montclair's 'bear hug' by claiming that it was initiating a new strategic review to consider multiple expressions of interests from a number of parties (according to Equal's public filings, nineteen parties had expressed interest in bidding for the company).

Meanwhile, Andrew Shapiro at Lawndale Capital, who had learned about Equal from my Seeking Alpha articles, had crossed the 4% ownership threshold and started to make some noise about what he thought was wrong with the company. Lawndale fired the first bullet by publishing a copy of a letter it wrote to Equal's board on April 2, in which it cited significant shortcomings in governance. Lawndale disagreed with a series of by-laws initiated by Equal for the clear purpose of further entrenching the board and management, and it disagreed with the issuance of potentially hundreds of thousands of additional dilutive shares in the form of options and grants to executives. Finally, the letter offered recommendations on how to respond to Montclair's buyout offer.

I was happy to see Lawndale join the fray. Andrew told me that he was considering filing his own 13D and that a proxy contest was not out of the question. As he was in a position to do what I was prevented from doing, I was determined to give him all the help he needed, and sent him a list of Equal's key shareholders and their contact information. Andrew was going to Equal's AGM on May 13 and said that, to his surprise, no other major shareholder had shown any interest in meeting with him. I decided to go—to meet him, and to further encourage him to pursue my activist agenda.

(I also had the idea of attending the AGM, wearing duct tape marked 'censored' on my mouth, or wearing a 'V for Vendetta' mask, but my lawyer advised against it.)

Andrew and I met at the Calgary airport. Andrew was a tall balding man in his 50s. We shook hands, grabbed a cab and went for dinner. As we sat on the patio of the River Café on Prince's Island Park, Andrew told me about himself, about his extensive activism background and his activism philosophy. When we moved on to the Equal case, he had a long list of prepared questions, some stemming from previous discussions we have had over the phone, we also came up with other items worth exploring at the next morning AGM. For example, I told him that if he mentioned the possibility of converting Equal to an MLP, Equal's management/board would say that an MLP structure would penalize Canadian shareholders from a tax standpoint, and that his response should be: "Canadian shareholders won't complain if such a conversion would lead to a doubling of the share price." (That exact exchange between Andrew and Dan Botterill took place the following day). The question of Equal's conversion to a Master Limited Partnership became even more pertinent after New Source Energy Partners went public in February 2013. New Source was almost an exact replica of Equal Energy: the company operated exclusively in the Hunton formation, it produced about 60% of Equal's output in terms of barrels per day, but its production was more liquids-weighted, meaning that it's cash flow was similar to Equal's despite having lower production. New Source adopted exactly the same model that Adam and I had advocated for Equal, which consisted of maintaining flat production and using cash flow to pay a generous dividend. By following this model, New Source enjoyed a valuation that was up to three times higher than Equal's. Feeling confident that Andrew was going to press management the next day, I took a flight back to Vancouver the same evening.

The next day, Equal held its annual shareholder meeting. After a lengthy presentation by the management to rally the shareholder base and defend their hostile action against shareholders, they opened the floor to questions. Based on the accounts of shareholders who attended the meeting, the board and the management took a lot of heat for their actions; the AGM environment was seemingly much more hostile to the board and management than during the shareholder meeting I attended in the prior year. However, the vote taken at the meeting was the real vindication for the activism campaign. The voting result was a shameful defeat to Equal's management and board; the legacy directors barely crossed the 50% affirmative vote benchmark. (Adam and I, despite owning 5% of the company, were prohibited from voting—had we been allowed to vote, no legacy director would have reached the 50% approval threshold.) Klapko received the lowest total—50.77%, a dismal result, by any measure, for any CEO. Those dismal results were obtained while Kingsdale was still retained as a proxy solicitor and all the directors were running unopposed.

Furthermore, shareholders universally rejected all proposals advanced by the board, including the 'advanced notice' provision. This provision was put forth in conjunction with the lawsuit filed in January and was designed to further entrench and protect the board from future challenges by shareholders. The rejection of that measure was a major coup for shareholders. Finally, the board failed to pass a resolution to issue additional unallocated options and restricted shares to the company's executives, which was yet another slap in the face of Equal's management team.

It was at this AGM that three of the seven board members were replaced: Dan Botterill, Roger Giovanetto and Peter Carpenter. Carpenter and Giovanetto were the longest-serving directors; under their watch, Equal's stock price declined from $46.83 on the day they joined the board (May 18, 2006) to $3.71 on the day of their exit—a decline of 92%. Dan Botterill's record was a tad better—when he joined the board on May 12th 2011, the stock was $7.12, so he can be credited with a mere 48% decline.

The board changes were apparently designed to placate shareholders but, as is usually the case with Equal, the changes did not go far enough. The legacy directors and CEO, who had driven the company to its sad state, remained in the majority. Shareholders were refused access to the board and weren't permitted to co-select the new board members proposed for election (the three new members were all American: Michael Coffman, Kyle Travis and Lee Canaan). Yet the desire for change was so strong, the new board members still received 69% of the vote. On the other hand, it is unclear how much power those three had. As I subsequently learned, in March, in response to the Montclair bid, Equal formed a special committee to start a new strategic review process to decide on the future of the company. None of the newly-elected members served on that committee after their election in May.

It is worth remembering that the shareholders campaign against the company was suspended almost four months prior to the vote, yet shareholders stood by the campaign message and voted loudly against the company. Not only did the hiring of Kingsdale Communications not reverse the tide of shareholder discontent, it probably strengthened it. The genie was out the bottle. The retail shareholder base, with its limited resources, was able to organize itself and got awfully close to toppling an entrenched management team. While the victory was not complete, the company was better for it and the damage to the management and board was substantial.

In response to the negative vote, the company issued a sheepish press release on May 16, taking note of shareholders' frustration and promising to "enhance communication between the board and shareholders." I found the release sorely lacking; it was akin to a bloody dictator such as Syria's Bashar al-Assad promising the people of Syria more speeches as he bombed and burned their neighbourhoods.

Shortly after reading the press release, I wrote to the new chairman, Michael Doyle, noting his offer to improve communication with shareholders. The gist of my message was one of consolation, as I was both attempting to explain the underlying reasons behind shareholder frustration, and to engage him in a proper dialogue. Six days later, I received a letter from Equal's lawyers threatening renewed legal action against Adam and me. So much for a commitment to improved shareholder communication.

I decided to completely cut communications with the company, except for casual emails on the monthly anniversaries of the signing of the settlement agreement to remind them of the period left before I could resume my activism. Meanwhile, I was building my war chest for an eventual renewed fight to begin on June 19, 2014, when the standstill would expire.

Building that war chest yet again entailed making some unsavoury choices. History was repeating itself—there I was, fully invested in Equal, yet without sufficient capital to generate the type of returns needed for an eventual resumption of hostilities. Once again, I was limited to trading options or trading heavily on margin. Having been burned badly and repeatedly by options trading, I decided to go for the latter, despite its many perils.

By August, I had identified a number of potential trading/investment candidates and gradually started building a large stake in them, with my favourite undervalued equity being Calgary-based Longview Oil. Meanwhile, as my position in Equal proceeded to appreciate as a result of a continued increase in propane prices, my margin buying increased and I added other investments.

In the meantime, in an August 15 regulatory filing, Montclair raised its initial lowball offer by 18.75% to $4.75. On August 20, Equal rejected that offer and said it was still undertaking a comprehensive study of strategic alternatives.

By September, my equity portfolio had hit a new high and I was far from the dark days of the fall of 2012. However, my margin position had ballooned to a whopping $5 million. Once again, I gorged on debt as I strove to generate millions in returns in a short period. Even though my gains on my non-Equal assets stood at $1 million, and that was more than enough to finance a renewed activism campaign in 2014, I adjusted my goal to generating millions more so I could acquire a larger ownership interest in Equal and thus be more effective in my next round of pressure against the company.

In the meantime, on September 19, Montclair again raised its offer, to $4.85, and left the door open for a higher offer. Equal's board promptly rejected this offer and affirmed the continuation of its strategic review, with an anticipated conclusion date at the end of

September. Of course, this date came and went with Equal reporting no meaningful progress.

On October 31, 2013, the seventh anniversary of my father's passing, I became anxious that Equal would deliver a repeat of its catastrophic 2012 review conclusion. This time, I was heavily margined and had a tough choice to make—cut my other investments, or reduce my stake in Equal until the review was concluded. I chose to completely exit my position in Equal. Its stock was already trading at $5.00 a share, almost 50% higher than my purchase price, thus its valuation was much closer to its net asset value. I also figured that if Equal disappointed with its second strategic review conclusion, I would have the opportunity to acquire it at a much lower price and continue the fight from a stronger position. If the conclusion was successful, then my activist mission would also be successful and I could move on to greener pastures.

I began aggressively selling my shares with the goal of netting $4.50 per share, or just over $2 million in profit. Every morning, I placed a sell order; I had such a large position that the sale took over two weeks. Once you are a 13D filer, you are obliged to update your share count when you sell or buy 1% of the outstanding shares of a company, and I crossed that threshold on November 5. I had ten days to file my updated share count, and preferred to file once I was completely out. I feared that if Equal knew I was exiting, the board would stall the review and delay its conclusion, keeping shareholders hostage. Luckily, by November 15, I was able to sell my last block of shares and file my updated 13D—nine minutes before the deadline. After the sale, I repaid most of my margin debt, and used a small margin balance while I sat on the sidelines.

On Monday, November 18, the company issued a cryptic press release indicating that its strategic review was "successful". Oddly, the release did not include any details beyond the fact that Equal's board had possibly identified a viable solution and had entered into an exclusive negotiation with an un-named party. Perhaps the press release was an attempt to prop up the stock price, which was depressed due to my sale; perhaps it was to spite me, now that I was not a shareholder. If that was the case, it was another confirmation that management did not understand the purpose of my activism.

A friend asked if I was frustrated about selling my shares possibly days before a successful review conclusion. I said I was not; I said I would be ecstatic if shareholders were to prevail. My sale was the prudent move to make, considering the composition of my portfolio at the time. I believed that I had matured as an investor, and I had to respect the principles that allowed me to accumulate my fortune—avoiding excessive debt was also a key consideration. Also, while I had reaped great profit from my Equal investment and could possibly gain even more, my interest in Equal had evolved beyond a mere financial gain as I fought this activist battle, the moral victory was as meaningful as exiting at the best price.

On December 6, Montclair Energy issued a press release expressing its concern that Equal's board was not effectively conducting its strategic review and warning that it was considering the initiation of a special shareholder meeting and the nomination of independent directors. This was a clear indication that Montclair was frustrated, both as a shareholder and as a rejected potential suitor (I later found out that, on November 6, Montclair had made an offer of $5.40).

On Monday, December 9, Equal announced that it was being acquired by the private company Petroflow for $5.43 a share. It was a disappointing conclusion to an eighteen-month process of strategic reviews that cost millions in legal and banking fees. The company certainly did not have to sell itself; the original trust/MLP conversion plan that I proposed remained as valid, if not more so, considering higher commodities prices and the premium valuation enjoyed by the Hunton-focused MLP New Source Energy Partners. Alas, with my settlement restrictions in effect, and because I owned no shares at the time, there was little I could do.

Even though Equal shareholders received an annual dividend and eventually enjoyed a higher share price compared to when I commenced my activism, I was disappointed with the outcome of the latest strategic review. Adam was equally disappointed. He was still holding most of his original shares; upon hearing of this deal, he exited.

My empirical work with Adam indicated that, on the day the deal was announced, Equal's net asset value exceeded $6.80. So the company had, once more, short-changed its shareholders by agreeing to a deal at $5.43. At its peak, in July 2005, Equal's shares traded as high as $96.00. After years of mismanagement and a general decline in natural gas prices, attaining that price was out of the question. But the company could have continued as an ongoing concern, paying substantial dividends to shareholders under an income-focused trust or MLP, for decades.

The day Don Klapko was officially crowned as CEO and Director of the company, in June 2008, Equal Energy's shares traded at $14.37, or 264% higher than the special committee's agreed- upon deal price in December 2013. While Equal's shareholders took the brunt of the loss during his reign, Klapko was due to receive a golden parachute worth $3.4 million (according to the December 31st 2013 preliminary proxy circular). This is in addition to the $11.73 million in total compensation received by him between 2008 and 2012.

Equal's shareholders with many of whom I developed a close relationship, deserved better. But the system is stacked against the interests of the retail shareholder and it is mighty difficult to overthrow a well-entrenched board and management team. It is not impossible, but such an endeavour requires proper planning, a clear understanding of the legal maze associated with such a process, and plenty of resources to sustain a lengthy and contentious public fight.

Still, while changing a CEO and or replacing board members may be difficult, exposing corporate incompetence is not as hard as it used to be. Shareholders with a basic understanding of digital media and a shoestring budget may shake corporations to the core by shedding light on their behaviour and forcing them to change— sometimes, the knowledge that you are being observed is enough to change your behaviour. Shareholders should not be afraid of taking executives to task about immoral or selfish behaviour, and even those who don't have the power to create change should at least gather the courage to point.

As Edmund Burke famously stated, "All that is necessary for the triumph of evil is that good men do nothing." As long as shareholders shy away from exercising their right to police the people who govern the companies in which they invest, the higher the likelihood that corporate greed will triumph.

■ ■ ■

With the Equal activism finished, I had time to sit and reflect on my investment career. I have spent half my life wrestling with the markets so I could build a fortune and be free but, as time passed, it became clearer that chasing a fortune is an endless mirage. I found a purpose in activism, but I am still not sure if this is my true calling.

My personal life has always been intertwined with my business life. I have drawn from my life experience to be a better investor, and my investment and activism experience have taught me to be a better person. The harmony between the two can be a powerful force, because it offers a chance to channel life's energy into the pursuit of a singular goal. But this isn't always easy; when the barriers between work and personal life fall, the ups and downs of each can intrude on the other. In time, one may swallow the other.

When we are born, we are not given any sort of manual on how to live a happy and fulfilling life. Some of us find happiness in work, some in family, some in discovery, some in religion, some in love. We find happiness in what is meaningful to us. I have often used my work as a way to find meaning in my life, but I have learned that work is a way to stay alive, not a reason to be alive. While I continue to march on the path of an investor and activist, I know that investing and activism will be only part of my life—not my whole life.

I am proud of my investment accomplishments and my activism success (albeit partial), yet I can't help but ask if everything I've done has meaning—not because I doubt the validity of my personal and professional accomplishments, but because the meaning of life continues to elude me. While I know that my actions have touched the lives of many and may have meant a lot to them, I still do not know what we are living for. Nevertheless, I continue to find the energy to forge a path forward; perhaps because I have always known that, no matter what, the show must go on.

The End